HOW TO EAT
THE ELEPHANT

BUILD YOUR BOOK IN BITE-SIZED STEPS

ANN SHEYBANI

Summit Press Publishers
Canton, Connecticut

Copyright © 2015 by Ann Sheybani

Listen, you're going to find some mistakes in this book: some typos, an overzealous use of a comma or semicolon, that sort of thing. These things happen, even when you hire a professional editor. Pat yourself on the back if you find one, and remember that to err is human; to forgive, divine.

Summit Press Publishers
P.O. Box 759
Canton, Connecticut
860-306-4057
www.summit-success.com

Book Layout ©2014 Unauthorized Media
Ordering Information:

Quantity sales. Special discounts are available on quantity purchases by corporations, associations, and others. For details, contact the author at annsheybani@gmail.com

How To Eat The Elephant/ Ann Sheybani. —1st ed.

ISBN 978-0-9863309-0-2

To protect privacy, pseudonyms have been used in the student examples recounted.

Contents

Step Four: Staying Steady Through The Storm

Step Five: Publication For Dummies

For Walt, my best bud

I'd finally reached a point where the prospect of not writing a book was more awful than the one of writing a book that sucked. And so at last, I got to serious work on my book.

— *CHERYL STRAYED*

Introduction

Know how to eat an elephant? Yes, that's right, one small bite at a time. That's how you write a book, run a marathon, earn a college degree; how you accomplish any hairy, audacious goal worthy of your time and energy. You know that; everybody does. You know better than to contemplate massive goals in their entirety. You know that, in order to avoid paralysis and/or nervous breakdowns, you need to chunk the thing down into little pieces. After all, that's why you're holding this step-by-step guidebook in your sweaty little palms. A goal without a plan is just a wish. And you're done wishing.

Welcome. Welcome to that moment. You're about to take that first bite of elephant. You're about to turn your clever ideas into a real, live book. You're done talking about it; you just are. You've grown bored (along with everybody else) with all of those highly imaginative excuses you've concocted for not sitting down to write. The grout bleaching will just have to wait, and the closet rearranging, and the unicorn grooming. You're ready, finally, to turn those cocktail napkin musings into something beautiful and tangible. Plan in hand, you're ready to take action. You're going to start, right here, right now. We—you and I—are going to get this party started.

Not only are we going to begin, which is always the hardest part, we're going to keep the flow going in a very manageable, realistic way until you have in your hands—gasp!—a published book. We're going to build that book of yours, bite by bite, in five manageable steps.

What You Can Expect

Let me give you a brief overview of what we'll cover in this book. I just love brief overviews, don't you?

I'd like to begin by introducing you to some simple, get-your-ass-in-that-seat tools that will keep you writing, even when your pet unicorn whinnies for attention.

Then, before we explore the different types of books (genres) you might want to write, and the time and skill required for many of them; we're going to focus on the WHY. Why, pray tell, do you want to write this book? The Why always comes before the What (genre). Knowing your Why will allow you to make some informed decisions. Narrowing down the choices, such as picking a genre, will always help you avoid paralysis.

Hold on, because we're going to get really crazy around here. We'll talk about the writing process itself—what it actually looks like to take a project from concept to publication, as opposed to that fantasy you developed watching *Finding Forrester*. This may also be a good place to mention the timeframe required for completing a book. Contrary to what some Internet marketers would have you believe, writing a book, one that doesn't involve pet quotes, will likely take longer than 48 hours.

Once the dust settles, we'll begin the process of gathering content for your book. Not only will we create new material, we'll identify some stuff you may already have lying around. I'm sure you'd agree that there's nothing more satisfying than re-purposing pieces you, or someone you love, has already sunk big time into creating.

Of course, once we've got gobs of material to work with (I like to think of it as clay), it's time to begin forming bricks. Bricks—or stories—are the essential building blocks of a book. For any story to hold together properly, however, it needs to contain certain basic elements, which we'll discuss.

A huge pile of bricks is great, you say, but what am I supposed to do with them all? How will they all fit together in the end? No problem, because, for you worrywarts out there, we're going to develop an architectural blueprint for your book. This diagram, or outline, is going to show you where to place these separate bricks (stories), so you can create cohesion. We're also going to give your book a working title. By doing this, your book will feel alarmingly real, which will keep you motivated.

Did I mention the trouble you'll be running into along the way? Well, there will be barricades, barbed wire, and open manhole covers along the path. I think it best to plan for the inevitable, so you can overcome. We'll discuss tenacity, and doubt, and boredom, and being OK with your shitty first draft. We'll also talk about where to find continuing support; and how to identify fixes from other books when you begin the revision process; and that seemingly never-ending, lonely path ahead.

For those who prefer to see their musings in print sooner, rather than later, we'll explore the rather attractive option of hiring professionals to clean up your draft; where to find these angels of mercy, and how much their services generally cost.

Before we wrap things up, we're going to have a little church chat about the publishing industry. I'll explain the differences between traditional publishing, partnership publishing, and self-publishing. We'll talk about advances, and agents, and query letters, and platforms, and promotion and the wide-open vistas of this brave new world. We're going to talk about these things because you'll stay a whole bunch more motivated during the process. Even without an MFA or a ginormous fan base, you'll have lots of options for getting your work in print.

This Witty Coach Of Yours

Listen, I know all of your sorry excuses for not settling down to write your book, because I invented them. I know exactly how to start a novel, then shove it in the drawer at page 84. I know exactly how to complete the fourth draft of a memoir, then stick it in the closet behind that pair of jeans I can't wear anymore. I know how to write, and rewrite, and rewrite some more, then give up because I think the process should be so much easier. I know all about doubt, and fear, and procrastination, and perfectionism…. In other words, I've got your number, Sweetheart.

A long time ago, I realized I had a story to tell about the years I'd spent living in Iran with a staunch Muslim husband. Upon hearing my tale of intrigue and woe, people—well-intentioned friends, polite dinner companions, and blind dates—encouraged me to write a book. Buying into their enthusiasm, I went back to school at the age of thirty-eight to get a writing degree. From Harvard.

Early on, I had success publishing short stories and personal essays, which made the whole *writing thing* appear seductively easy. I thought I could toss some ideas on the page, juggle a few words, sharpen some verbs, and win a Pushcart Prize before the sun set. After I earned my Master's degree, I scurried home to begin my memoir. Five drafts later, I had a very different story than the one I'd first set out to write, which is a good thing, and yet it needed *something* more. I slowly recognized that *the writing thing* was tougher than it looked.

Years went by. I found myself at a prestigious writing conference meeting with agents and publishers. We chatted about the various requirements to sell a book—my book—to a big publishing house. Without a platform, query letter, or book proposal, it became clear that my book wouldn't be purchased, published, or promoted by any of the big New York City houses. Which explained the stunning lack of interest in the manuscript I was pitching. Mind you, this took place long before the traditional publishing industry collapsed, and all of those disinterested people lost their jobs. Not that I'm gloating or anything.

Times have changed, but some things have not. Regardless of the method of publication, writers still need a platform (an audience) if they want to sell their books. To build interest in my unpublished memoir, I began a blog, which, after a year or so, attracted some followers. My husband also began a blog, the content of which he eventually turned into a book. After I forgave him for finishing his project first, we set to work with a lovely partnership press to edit, design, publish, and promote his book, which we'll talk about later.

For the last several years, I've been running The East Hill Writers' Workshop with a couple of talented partners. We've sat back and watched folks turn pages of scribble into 400-page manuscripts. We've also seen writers give up in the middle of their first draft, to turn their attention to another project the moment they run into an obstacle. Then, after their next false start, throw their hands up in the air and just give up because writing a book was supposed to be quick and easy. Crazy as that sounds, it happens all the time.

I began my practice as a writing coach, not just because I like bossing people around, which I do, but also because I know all of the ridiculous excuses writers use to screw themselves up. I dig browbeating creative types just like you into developing a consistent writing practice, and getting their work out the door. The way I see it, my job is to kick your tail until you complete the first shitty draft because, with the exception of starting the project in the first place, that's the hardest part of the process. It doesn't matter if it takes you six weeks, or six months, or six years, your mission is to get this shitty first draft completed so you'll have in your hands the one thing that separates you from the dreamers: something tangible to work with. Then, and only then, can you begin revising the thing; then choosing a method of publication.

So, yah; I know. I know each and every obstacle and excuse for not writing a book, because I've smacked into them, and used them myself. Sorry, you can't outfox me.

Before we get going, before we get real, we need to take care of a little business. I need you to make a commitment, not to me, but to yourself.

Your Hollow Pledge

I _____ do solemnly declare and accept that I am a procrastinator who is afraid of work, and the very thought of failure. And I want to do something about it. I promise not to waste any more valuable time by surfing the net, or watching reruns of *Get Smart*, or clipping coupons. I will no longer be seduced by shortcuts and promises of overnight success. I will stop making excuses. I will haul my rump off the sofa and set it down in front of my computer, and I will type. I will type and type and type until I've got myself a shitty first draft.

I understand that my J-O-B is to complete a shitty first draft. I got it! And only after that will I contemplate revision, then publication. I understand there will be obstacles, and blood.

I swear on my mother's life (or my children's) to do as my witty writing coach tells me and at all times to retain my sense of humor.

Signed:

Dated:

Now go on, get going. Turn the page. And for God's sake, loosen up and have some fun! This won't hurt much. I promise.

STEP ONE

ON YOUR MARK, GET SET, GO

CHAPTER ONE

Preparing for Greatness

It's time to prepare for greatness. How does one do that, you ask?

First things first: Writers need structure. This was a hard lesson for me to learn because I hate structure. See, I like to be freewheeling. I dig going with the flow, the wind streaming through my hair, and seeing where the road takes me. Don't fence me in is my favorite motto. But this philosophy causes me problems as a writer. For a writer, freedom can be our worst enemy. It can lead to paralysis, procrastination, aimlessness, and indecision. Now, the problem with creating structure for us whimsical types is that it doesn't just happen on its own because we hope it will. We have to develop some very particular practices and commit to them. We can't just give them lip service.

It's time to get organized and make writing a priority in your life.

It's also time to set some SMART goals. SMART stands for: *S*pecific, *M*easurable, *A*ctionable, *R*ealistic, and *T*ime-defined. Here's an example of a SMART goal: I will write at least twenty pages of my book by Friday evening of this week. It's specific, those twenty pages; and actionable, unless your hands get cut off; and realistic, unless you actually can't write or type; and time-defined, what with you finishing up by Friday night. Here's an example of a stupid goal: I really should get to my book this week, if I can break away from The Shopping Network. You see the difference? Thought so.

To develop that necessary structure, we're going to do three things:

1.   **Take out your calendar.**

It doesn't matter if your calendar is the old-fashioned paper variety, or if it's the online type. (Personally, I love gCal with its nagging alarm reminders.) We're going to begin by setting some writing appointments for the week; some SMART appointments.

Because the mind works best when you can focus, uninterrupted, on a task for a reasonable amount of time—not too little, and not too long, something just right for you and your untreated ADHD—we'll create some blocks. It may take a session or two to get the feel for which time block works best for you, but for now, choose between the following: Two 3-hour writing sessions per week, or three 2-hour writing sessions per week.

Now, pen these into your calendar, in blood. Will you write from 8:00 to 10:00 a.m. on Monday, Wednesday, and Friday? Or will you write from 9:00 p.m. to midnight on Saturday and Sunday? Choose. You know best what will work with your hectic schedule; what time of day your brain functions optimally. You can reasonably predict when the kids, or the dog, or your partner will be otherwise occupied. (By the way, this is a great time to draw some healthy boundaries around you and your dreams; to teach your loved ones that there are certain times when you'll be unavailable, unless, of course, someone has broken their leg.)

I happen to be a morning person. I'm at my best before noon. I like to write three times a week, just after I go for my morning run. That's when ideas tend to flow for me. That's when I have time and space to think, when I'm least likely to be interrupted.

But you may be a night owl. You might prefer to sit down

at midnight and lose yourself to the sound of the ticking clock. Maybe you stay focused for three hours at a time because that's how you roll. Maybe two hours work best for you because you get tired and want to hit the hay.

You know yourself. Follow your own rhythms. What works for other people may not work for you.

Regardless, six hours a week is a manageable goal, and realistic. You don't have to quit your day job to fit your writing time in, nor do you have to give up your friends and family, even if you'd sometimes like to.

Be forewarned: Without regular writing appointments, you will wander off, dragging out the process of writing a book for years on end.

2.   **Get a notebook exclusively for your story ideas.**

When you write consistently, ideas will begin to come to you when you least expect them. The unconscious mind becomes your little unpaid helper. Buy a notebook, any kind you like, and carry it with you everywhere you go, even out to dinner or to church. Someone clever, or really dumb, will say something to spark your imagination, and, man, you'll want to capture that. Or suddenly, that line of dialogue, or that aspect of character, or that supporting argument you've been struggling with will magically appear. Fail to write it down, and it will evaporate into thin air. If you feel uncomfortable scribbling in the presence of others, particularly among those who sigh a lot, excuse yourself and run to the nearest restroom. Whatever it takes, just get the good stuff down, before it's lost to the ether.

When you read other books and get a flash of inspiration, jot those ideas down in your story notebook as well.

Now, here's where the regular practice comes in. Right before bed, or first thing in the morning, make some notes in your story notebook. Do this every day, even if you've captured something fabulous while out and about. I promise it will become a habit you'll not want to give up. Like brushing your teeth.

The notes you jot down can include questions: How am I going to weave in the backstory of my protagonist's first marriage? Or random ideas: Write about the streets of Abadan in as much detail as possible. Or thoughts about structure: Maybe I should switch up the narrator in alternating chapters, first Doris, then Biff.

We're going to come back to the story notebook when we discuss creating content. Right now, you're digging a well from which to draw.

3.   **Get a separate notebook for your Morning Pages.**

Morning Pages are three pages of longhand, stream of consciousness writing, done first thing in the morning. This tool, developed by Julia Cameron of *The Artist's Way*, is the best method I know to clear your head for the day. If you haven't read her book, you should.

Here's how it works: Before your day gets busy, before you take your shower or fiddle with breakfast, sit with a devoted notebook and jot down three pages of random thoughts. Write whatever comes to mind: A note to pick up the dry cleaning, some thoughts on that fool at the office who stole your stapler, a description of the hors d'oeuvres you want to serve at your dinner party.... Get the garbage swirling around in your head onto the page. Forget about editing; or worrying about grammar or spelling: Let your pen move rapidly across the page from start to finish. By doing this, not only do you open your creative channels so you can better focus on your project, you also experience a useful mode of writing, free of the impulse to edit. We'll talk about the dangers of "editing in the field" before the proverbial sun has set.

Why, Why, Why, Why, Why

Can I ask you a question? Why do you want to write a book? Seriously, do you even know? What is your purpose for doing so?

- To create a beautiful work of art?

- To tell your life story?

- To outline your message?

- To serve as an expert calling card?

- To give you recognition as an expert?

- To instruct in a straightforward, how-to manner?

- To impact other people's lives and affect radical change?

- To improve your business status, marketability, and profitability?

Because your Why for writing this book—and you have to be very honest with yourself, Pumpkin—will help determine what type of book you'll write, what genre. You'll see in the next chapter that you've got lots of choices, and you'll need to pick one lickety-split, or you'll end up twiddling your thumbs instead of starting.

Here's the deal: If you want to create a beautiful piece of art, to have someone finish your book, set it down in their lap, and dream for days about the power of your words, the unforgettable images, that character seared into her psyche, you're not going to write a how-to book, at least not likely.

If you'd like to outline your message and be seen as an expert in your field, you'd be silly to write a novel, unless you're hankering to pen a parable. (A parable is a short(ish) story that illustrates a moral attitude or religious principle, an example of which is Bob Berg's *The Go-Giver*.)

If you want to explain how your mother's knitting obsession ruined your childhood, despite making you the man you are today, you've got a couple of options, which we'll discuss in a moment.

There is no "right" motivation for writing a book; it's different for everybody. Be brutally honest with yourself. It's OK to want to be seen as an expert, not an artist. You can yearn to tell your life story, not teach a useful skill, without labeling yourself a first-class narcissist. Don't make life harder for yourself by ignoring your real motivation. Truth is good.

Writing a book is a process. From time to time, you'll question yourself and the relevance of your words. Other people will offer suggestions or opinions that will stir up doubt. Go back to your Why. Use it as a touchstone to ground yourself.

CHEW ON THIS

1. Take out your calendar. Commit to and schedule two 3-hour sessions, or three 2-hour sessions this week. You'll be doing this each week for the foreseeable future. Nurture the habit. Don't make me repeat myself.

2. Buy two notebooks: One for your stories, and one for your morning pages.

3. Each morning, write three Morning Pages to flush your mental toilet.

4. Each evening, make a few notes in your story notebook to keep your project percolating.

5. Answer this question in sickening detail: I want to write this book for/because…

6. And this one: I want my readers to understand…

CHAPTER TWO

Choosing Your Genre

Armed with your Why, it's time to decide on a genre for your book. Before you can make a reasonable decision, one you're not going to constantly waffle back and forth on, we'll need to do a little browsing first. Let's sift through the racks here, and I'll identify and describe a few of the options, give you some examples of each. You might notice at first blush that some of these book types seem a lot more complicated to write than others. And you would be correct. Hold your fears in abeyance, however, and we'll get to all that.

This is by no means a complete list of genres, but it'll get you started thinking.

Types Of Books And Examples

Quotations
The Little Book of Romanian Wisdom by Diana Doroftei
Life: Selected Quotes by Paulo Coelho

Workbooks
Boundaries Workbook: When to Say No and When to Say Yes by

Henry Cloud
The Self-Esteem Workbook by Glenn Shiraldi

Anthologies
The Right Words at the Right Time by Marlo Thomas
A Blessing in Disguise by Andrea Joy Cohen

Motivational
Simple Grace by Beth Jannery
The Art of Exceptional Living by Jim Rohn

Instructional/ How-to
The Secrets of Skinny Chicks by Karen Bridson
Design Your Self by Karim Rashid

Expert Positioning
Journeys on the Edge: Living a Life that Matters by Walt Hampton
Own Your Niche by Stephanie Chandler

Self-help
Feel the Fear and Do it Anyway by Susan Jeffers
Fearless Living by Rhonda Britten

Humor
Let's Pretend This Never Happened by Jenny Lawson
Sh*t My Dad Says by Justin Halpern

Travel
A Walk in the Woods by Bill Bryson
A Year in Provence by Peter Mayle

Memoir
Eat, Pray, Love by Elizabeth Gilbert
Traveling Mercies by Anne Lamott

Novel (followed by some of the subsets)

Little Bee by Chris Clive
Gone with the Wind by Margaret Mitchell

Romance
The Pirate Lord by Sabrina Jeffries
Confessions of a Scoundrel by Karen Hawkins

Science Fiction
The Atlantis Gene by A.G. Riddle
The Martian by Andy Weir

Horror
The Shining by Stephen King
Joe Dies at the End by David Wong

Thriller
Never Go Back by Lee Child
Ripper by Isabel Allende

Western
The Walking Drum by Louis L'Amor
The Light of Western Stars by Zane Grey

Short Story Collection
Interpreter of Maladies by Jumpha Lahiri
Birds of a Lesser Paradise by Megan Mayhew Bergman

Poetry Collection
Hidden Drive by Chivas Sandage
School of the Arts by Mark Doty

Young Adult Novel
The Hunger Games by Suzanne Collins
Harry Potter by J.K. Rowling

Middle Grade Novel
Beezus and Ramona by Beverly Cleary

Hello God, It's Me Margaret by Judy Blum

Children's Book
The Rainbow Fish by Marcus Pfister
The Velveteen Rabbit by Margery Williams

Which Door Will It Be?

So how do you decide on a genre, what with there being so many of them to choose from? I'm going to introduce a few questions you'll want to ask yourself to help you narrow down the options. I want you to think about your answers as I go along.

Is my story best told in the long or short form?

Let me break this down a little for you. How big is the story you want to tell? If it involves several characters—your Mom, Uncle Buck, all fifteen of your cousins—you might want to think in terms of a longer form: a memoir, or a novel if you realllllyyyyy don't want to name names.

The short form, by contrast, allows you, the writer, to focus on specific, tiny moments in which things or relationships change. Like that money conversation you had with your ex-fiancé, Lydia. (Bet you learned a lot from that incident!) Or that time you drove your Subaru into the reservoir, which ended up costing you big time. Perhaps you'd like to put together a collection of personal essays about your financial lessons instead of writing a memoir, or a collection of funny short stories, rather than a novel.

Is my story meant to be fiction or nonfiction? Novel or memoir?

Does your story hold more power when told through a clear but meaningful exploration of truth? Does it absolutely matter that your mother made you deliver Avon orders on your bike when you were a kid, which prompted your drug use? That it was she, and Avon Incorporated, not anybody else, who catalyzed your Advil addiction, thereby ruining your life? Then go memoir.

Perhaps your story would hold more power through the creation of situations or characters that are imagined, where you're not tied to the facts. Then a novel could be the way to go. If you'd like to take something that really happened but go further with it—use the incident as a leaping off point—go with the novel. Deliver the Avon orders on your bike, but then ride off into the sunset to join the circus.

If you're torn between fiction and non-fiction, you can always choose a scene—riding your bike while the neighborhood boys taunt you—and write it in each form. In which form, fiction or non-fiction, does it seem most compelling? Is it more interesting when Mom ignores your humiliation and distress, or when your bike spokes decapitate the loudest bully?

What if I haven't taken a writing class since 1974?

Here are some basic things to consider: If you have very little experience with writing—and remember, we'll be talking about how to write as we go along, and who can help you clean things up when you're done—you may want to consider some very simple non-fiction structures:

- A collection of quotes

- A motivational book that makes a series of simple, supported points

- A how-to guide

And before you go and dismiss such books as tripe, I'd like to point out the September 1, 2013 edition of the *New York Times Book Review*. *Grumpy Cat*—written by a brother and sister team who are currently making more money than God—was listed at number 10 on the Motivational and How-to Bestseller List.

On Amazon, this is how *Grumpy Cat* is described:

"Internet sensation Grumpy Cat's feline frown has inspired legions of devoted fans. Celebrating the grouch in everyone, the *Grumpy Cat* book teaches the fine art of grumpiness and includes enough bad attitude to cast a dark cloud over the whole world. Featuring brand new as well as classic photos, and including grump-inspired activities and games, *Grumpy Cat* delivers unmatched, hilarious grumpiness that puts any bad mood in perspective."

If you want to see how simple the concept is, find *Grumpy Cat* on Amazon and take a look inside! You don't have to write *The Grapes of Wrath*, or *Eat, Pray, Love* to have a literary and/or financial success on your hands.

Finally, if you haven't figured this out already, memoirs and novels require a lot more knowledge of the writing craft. Things can get ugly PDQ if you don't know the difference between plot and setting. Further down the road, we'll talk about the basics of craft. I'm going to spend lots of time spelling things out for you braver folks, but for now, I'm going to move things along.

What if I only have a weekend to get this thing done?

Here's the deal. Can you write a book in a weekend the way many programs promise? The answer is yes, and no. Let me explain.

The answer is yes if you have a lot of readily available material. You can take content that you've already created—blog pieces or workshop materials or your college thesis—and string them together into a very loose structure. The key concept here, of course, is that you already have lots of written material. The next step would be to cut and paste and figure out in which order your content makes the most sense, offers the best flow. This could take you, if you're not too choosy, 48 hours.

If you're a smart cookie, you'd then send your manuscript to a line editor and pay her $1200 to fix the spelling, punctuation, and grammar, and to point out the redundancies before you self-publish. Or pay a partnership press some good money to clean the thing up, then publish it. (We'll be talking about editors and the various publishing options later.)

Here's another way you can write a book in a weekend. Let's not forget the beautiful example of *Grumpy Cat*. You can also take loads of pictures of your cat or dog, then write clever quotes in bubbles above its head. Providing your pet is particularly cooperative, you could have yourself a book by sunset on Sunday.

Mind you, you'd want to hire an editor and a format designer to handle the array of clever pictures before you self-publish, or turn those tasks over to a partnership press.

Another perfectly legitimate option is to create an anthology. An anthology is a collection of essays or short stories that others have submitted to you. As the collection editor, your job would be to piece them all together in a logical order. You'd also be responsible for hiring the line editor or the partnership press to make it clean and beautiful.

The answer is HELL NO, you can't write a book in a weekend, if you're starting from scratch, particularly if you're looking to write the next greatest American novel.

By the way, if your desire is to make money and pay your mortgage before the bank forecloses on you and your hungry kids, you don't want to write a novel or a memoir. These types of books, with rare exceptions, are quite involved. They take more time and effort to write than any of the other genres. (Another great reason you need to be clear on your Why.)

I've always wanted to write a book like _____, so can I copy it without getting into trouble?

Some people know exactly the sort of book they'd like to write, making the previous questions seemingly irrelevant. I can't tell you the number of adventurous women I run into who want to create another *Eat, Pray, Love*, a three-part memoir about running away from grief and reinventing one's self abroad. They're chomping at the bit to describe their Parisian love affair, or that stint in Iceland breeding Puffins, or their brush with enlightenment in the Amazon. (The jungle, silly, not the online vendor.) They've got a very specific vision that looks an awful lot like Elizabeth Gilbert's.

If you've got a book like this in mind, that's fabulous. In fact, we're going to spend a good deal of time exploring the modeling concept. That's why I'm going to ask you to shop around for a book you'd like to "recreate," even if you pride yourself on being original. (Don't worry. I promise you'll keep your integrity in tact.)

OK. You've had a chance to answer some important questions.

Now it's time to stop being overwhelmed by choice. Knock it off, already, and pick your genre.

AN ASSIGNMENT FROM YOUR COACH

I want to remind you of a number of important concepts. As your coach, I see it as my job to give you an occasional tap on the nose to make sure you've got your head in the game. Ready?

1. You're a writer. That means you need to read other writers. Turn off the TV and read!

2. The only way to begin is simply to begin. I wish it were more complicated.

3. Tell the story in the first format that occurs to you. If, after you've finished your first draft, it seems wrong to have told your life story in the how-to form, then turn it into something else. But only after you've finished. Trust me on this one: Nothing is a waste.

4. Writing is a pleasure. A little luxury. Like eating an ice-cream sundae, without the calories. You can buy into the it's-so-damn-hard mindset, but you're only wasting precious energy and time. Coal mining is hard; writing, not so much. Let's keep this in perspective.

5. You get to do this. Look around. There's nobody holding a gun to your head. I hope.

6. Trust in the process. And we're going to talk a lot more about process. Every first draft, no matter who creates it, looks like garbage. It will get better. This is the starting point. Your book will change over time.

Why Waiting For Motivation Is Futile

Do you need to be motivated to take action? Nope. In fact, there are lots of times you'll absolutely NOT feel like taking action when you promised yourself you would sit down and write. These very moments, I'm here to tell you, are the moments you'll need to take action anyway. Otherwise you'll stand around filing your nails while the world passes you by.

I love writing, I really do, but I'd rather clean toilets than sit down to face a blank page. Actually, I'd rather trot down to the kitchen and eat the pan of raw vegan brownies my writing student just brought me. And I'd rather dig into season two of *House of Cards* on Netflix, which I've just discovered, and forget about the fact that I don't have a clue what I'm going to say next, preferably with the aforementioned brownies. But I digress.

Motivation, *i.e.* good feelings, is not required to take action. You act anyway, regardless of how uninspired you feel. Think of motivation as a perk, sort of like popcorn at the movies. Nice to have, particularly with a crapload of salt and butter, but not necessary to enjoy the show.

More often than not, motivation arises after you start, after you get going. After you start to write and get in the flow. And suddenly you don't know why you didn't want to start earlier. You feel good; you're motivated; you're on fire. The motivation, the good feelings, followed the action. Here's the funny thing: Motivation and action are co-arising phenomena. One doesn't necessarily precede the other. Sometimes, like when you've got lots of time and space, you can hardly wait to get going. Sometimes you can write for an hour and it feels like a day. That happens. It will happen.

So how do you take action during block time when you don't really feel like it, or if the motivation hasn't come somewhere during the process?

Remember your Why: Why you're working on this book in the first place. Dial back into the goal, the vision, the destination. The very reason you decided action was required in the first place. Connect regularly with your Why.

Decide you're going to do something once—like write for

two hours three times a week. Don't revisit your decision to act; don't bitch; don't re-think; don't re evaluate. Just do it.

Make it a habit; make it routine. Write from 9 p.m. to 11 p.m. on Thursday and Saturday nights. Be predictable. And boring. It's good for you.

Stop waiting around for the perfect moment, when you feel like it. For all of the planets to align and the angels to show up singing a show tune. The people who are getting the results you want? Who are doing the things you wish you could be doing? They're not riding the motivation pony, man. They're following a routine and doing the things they don't feel like doing. That's just how it works.

CHEW ON THIS

1. Choose one genre. There are no mistakes. This is the draft you'll complete.

2. Shop for and buy the book that best represents your vision.

3. Remove one time sink from your weekly schedule, like that mindless television series or that Facebook game, so you can create a writing block. Erase that PTO bake sale, or the neighborhood pig roast, or the shopping spree with your girlfriend.

CHAPTER THREE

The Writing Process, For Real

Before we set to work creating and gathering content, I'd like to pause, take a deep breath, and talk about the writing process. Believe me, you'll want to know what to expect so you can recognize the obstacles for what they are, inevitable pains in the ass. You'll want to know that what you're experiencing is normal, not some sign that you're doing something horribly wrong.

The One Draft Mentality

Beware the One Draft Mentality: That crazy notion that allows one to believe that a story can be captured on paper in one foul swoop. This perfectionistic, crippling mindset will prevent nice people like you from moving on to paragraph two before the next millennium.

Simply put, in order to write a book, you'll need to write several drafts, not just one, so do yourself a favor and just get over it.

But here's the good news: Your only job at this point is to write the first draft, the first shitty draft. This is THE big hurdle. The rest, relatively speaking, is cake. While you work on your shitty first draft, do not play with your wording, or polish your verbs, or restructure your sentences. Do not edit in the field, as landscape photographers say. Write. Just write. Get the stuff down as fast as it'll come. Because chances are really good that you're going to chop your first four chapters, or the first four pages of each chapter before you're done. Don't waste time on things that will likely go bye-bye.

I want to tell you a little story about my daughter, Iman, and her One Draft Mentality in order to anchor in my point. I'm going to paint a scene, because, as we'll discuss, scenes are what readers remember.

Not long ago, Iman came home for semester break with a 25-page paper due the day she was to return to class. True to her nature, Iman left her project until the very last minute. Stressed, she sat at the kitchen counter facing a blank piece of paper. She'd write one sentence, then think for ten minutes. She'd get up and pace, then sit back down to cry. Wiping her nose, she'd write the next belabored sentence before beginning the cycle again. This went on for hours. Bent over, her long, curly hair wet with tears, her tiny face pressed into hands no bigger than a baby's, she said, in response to my incredulous expression, "Mom, you don't understand. I don't have time to get this wrong."

See, Iman believes that it's a waste of time, that it's inefficient, to write multiple drafts of a paper. She believes that one should be able to get the job done, perfectly, in just one go. And to be fair, after fourteen hours of stress, after buckets of tears, she finished her paper, handed it in, and received a decent grade.

Like Iman, you might get away with the One Draft Mentality when writing a 25-page academic paper. Adopt that mindset when writing an entire book, however, and you'll end up in the psychiatric ward of your local hospital.

This is why I'm not only giving you permission to write a shitty first draft, I'm actually insisting that you do so. Now, when I say shitty first draft, I'm talking about writing so bad that you'd die of embarrassment if anyone read it, even the dog. Complete this draft first, then, and only then, go back and clean it up.

Listen; if you want to be really good at something, you must be willing to be bad in the beginning. That's how this thing called *process* works.

And while I'm doling out permission—permission designed to free you up, to allow your creativity to flow without that vicious self-judgment getting in the way—I'd like to offer you more:

I Hereby Give You Permission To Do The Following:

- You get to change your mind (after you write your shitty first draft)
- You get to make mistakes
- You get to vacillate
- You get to take your own sweet time
- You get to speak your mindt
- You get to be direct and honest
- You get to fail
- You get to be wrong
- You get to be "unreasonable"
- You get to shine
- You get to disengage yourself from problems you cannot immediately solve
- You get to play big
- You get to ask for help
- You get to be imperfect
- You get to be free
- You get to love yourself
- You get to leave things alone
- You get to experiment
- You get to question the *status quo*
- You get to have things the way you want them
- You get to rock the boat
- You get to be the wonderful, quirky you

The Cold Hard Truth

For some strange reason, whenever I conduct a beginners' writing workshop, one of my students invariably raises her hand and gushes on about her desire to write novels just like Jane Austen's. Jane Austen, I insist on mentioning, did not roll out of bed one morning at the tender age of twenty-five and write *Pride and Prejudice* in one go.

Prodigy or not, here are a few things you too should probably know about Jane Austen, and what she did in order to produce some decent books:

1. She wrote stories from the time she was a young child.

2. She lived in her parents' home until she died at forty-one, never having married.

3. Her family had money, so Jane could spend her days writing in her bedroom, not darning socks.

4. She wrote multiple drafts of her novels and threw away hundreds, if not thousands of pages, before she produced her masterpieces.

5. Her masterpieces weren't considered masterpieces until long after her death.

6. Jane Austen put in over 10,000 hours at her desk to become a master.

> **NOTE:**
> In his book *Outliers*, Malcolm Gladwell theorizes that true mastery—mastery of any skill—requires 10,000 hours of practice. In other words, no one comes out of the box writing like John Updike. Now, I'm not convinced that 10,000 hours is a prerequisite for a great book; but I do know that you need to give yourself permission to wrestle with this thing.

(For those of you who do not want to put in 10,000 hours in order to create a decent book, we'll be talking about editing services in a bit.)

Stay with me while I expand on this topic.

Have you ever watched a professional runner run? Looks so easy, doesn't it? They've all got that half smile playing across their face, that healthy sheen, those long, fluid strides that make the act seem so fun. From the couch, you can practically feel the endorphins pumping through your own body.

Inspired, you go out for a jog and discover that, instead of gliding like Flo Jo across the savannah, the wind whipping through your hair, you're ready to throw up by the end of the block. You shake your head, confused, because you know nothing about the inglorious stages a runner must go through along the way. You figure if something so simple feels so hard, there's got to be something wrong with you. Clearly, you've inherited your mother's delicate genes, not to mention her chunky thighs, so you might as well stagger back home and take up bridge.

No surprises here, good writing is a lot like good running. There's a lot more to the sport than meets the eye.

Just for a moment, I'd like to lift the skirts on writing and describe, in great detail, the "normal" process—the process that your favorite writers make look so deceptively easy. It's important to know what's really under there, so you'll know what to expect. For fun, I'm going to break the process down into thirteen predictable stages, or steps.

1. You start with a brilliant idea for an essay, or a chapter, and you can hardly wait to get going because you're really excited. You know exactly what you want to say. You can envision the perfect words pouring onto the paper while you sit back with your arms folded and witness the magic.

2. Grinning, you sketch out the story of a man you met who changed your life. Maybe you don't know exactly how he changed your life, but you recount all the memorable details: how you met, what he looked like, what he said, what you said, even the kind of cologne he wore. Lots and lots of great details.

3. You write page after page until you reach the end and you're ready to come to a conclusion. This man changed my life because...because....

4. You think back and you're suddenly not sure how he changed your life, or that he even did, or why you chose to write about him in the first place, or what anything you wrote about means, when push comes to shove. A trickle of sweat slides down your neck.

5. After you get your third glass of water, or eat the contents of your refrigerator, you sit back down and think some more. What was the point? Because there is a God in heaven and (S)He is merciful, you suddenly realize the story is about something else entirely, something crucial. You just need to change a few things, now, get rid of some stuff that was supporting the original aborted idea. You had no idea you were such a genius!

6. You flesh out your new point. It's really good.

7. Then you go back to the beginning of the piece and you realize that the story *really* starts on page four, which means you've got to cut those first four pages off—the ones, let's be honest, that took so damn much effort and time to write. (Because you don't waste, and we'll talk more about this later, you stick those extraneous pages in the Scrap Heap, a separate file in your computer labeled as such, and continue on your way.)

8. When you've got your story down, and you're feeling satisfied, you stick the draft in the bottom drawer. Even though you've been told not to edit in the field—not to go back and incessantly toy with your wording before your shitty first draft is done—you're going to ignore my instructions, and go back in to reevaluate, instead of pushing forward on your next story.

9. At first glance, you think that what you've got in hand looks pretty damn good. You're a natural. A genius. Oh, how you snort.

10. The next day, however, because you *really* can't follow instructions, you look at it again. You can't believe what's happened! Seemingly overnight, some cruel six-year-old got into your document and turned your brilliance into complete and utter shit. You weep. Profusely. And threaten to quit.

11. On Wednesday, always on Wednesday, you fix a few things because you just can't move on. Just because you have nothing better to do, now that you're a total, irredeemable failure, you slip in that random idea that popped in your head when you were picking up the dry cleaning, the one you should have written down in your story notebook instead. And suddenly the project, once again, kicks to life.

12. Finally, on Thursday, you figure your piece is good enough, once again, to move on to the next section. You keep your head down, and you claim, should anybody ask, that you'd never edit in the field because you understand your goal is to push forward so you can complete a shitty first draft full of horrors and mistakes. You bristle at the suggestion you could be so stupid.

13. And to make a long, sad story short, by the time you finish your final draft—that draft you'll mail out for publishing—you will have thrown out half of your chapters, or cut out enormous chunks of brilliance from one area and moved them to another. And that book of yours—its structure, its message, its tone—is nothing like what you envisioned in the beginning. It looks almost nothing like your shitty first draft, that draft you had to write to get to this point.

Here's the good news, the take-home message: You do not have to write a perfect first draft, like Iman. You don't even need to write a good one. In fact, consider it your job to write a Truly SHITTY First Draft. Because you just have to start.

You must start somewhere; or you'll never get anywhere.

Heed my words. The book that you set out to write this first go round will not be the same book you end up with when you're done. You are, therefore, wasting your precious time fiddling with things as you move along. Get the ideas down, as rough as they are, and push forward. Don't edit in the field.

Remember, nothing is a waste—time; effort; those beautiful words you struggled to come up with, or received as a gift from the Universe. It's all part of the process.

You don't get to skip to the front of the line. You don't get to run like Flo Jo before placing 155th in your town's annual 5K. You don't get to write *Pride and Prejudice* without creating, first, an awful lot of crap. Everyone goes through this sequence, this process, including Jane Austen.

CHEW ON THIS

1. Copy these words in black magic marker— the bigger the better: My J-O-B is to write a shitty first draft. Now hang them on the wall next to your computer.

2. Create a Scrap Heap folder on your computer. This is where the stuff you chop will end up. There will be excess, guaranteed.

3. Make a mistake this week. Tell people about it. Notice how you feel. Have a good laugh. Think about how you might do it differently next time.

CHAPTER FOUR

The Scavenger Hunt

Enough philosophy, let's get to work. Ready to start generating content for your book?

But wait! Before we create brand new material, seemingly out of thin air; we're going to identify some useful tidbits you may already have lying around. Look about. What are you ignoring? What could (and should) be included in your shitty first draft?

Not sure what I mean? I'll explain with a story.

Several years ago, my husband, Walt, got it into his head that he would start a blog. He began writing about the things he likes to think about: adventures, what he's learned from climbing mountains, God, meditation, books he's read, those sorts of things.

Each week he published a post, just like clockwork. After a year or two, an overarching message began to emerge, a philosophy if you will. He hadn't set out with this in mind, but it appeared nonetheless, which is exactly how a consistent writing practice works. The beauty of writing on a regular basis, particularly blogs, is that, by inadvertently writing about the same handful of topics, only in slightly different ways, your main lessons will discover you.

One day, Walt decided that, what with nothing better to do with his down time, it might be nice to write a book. He sat down at our dining table and began to organize his blog content. He read through each post, printed it out, then placed it into a thematic pile. Shuffling these groupings around, he began playing with different structures. What went where, he wondered. Was there, perhaps, a logical order? If he switched things around, putting this with that, that with this, would he create a different impact? He grew excited by the possibilities. He finished his shitty first draft, then revised the thing until he had what he wanted.

To make a long story short, nine months later, Walt published his book, *Journeys on the Edge: Living a Life that Matters*, with a wonderful partnership press out in Boise, Idaho.

The take-home point, you ask? The starting material for Walt's book was two years worth of single blog posts, 400-700 words long, which were just lying around.

Do you, my friend, have such a treasure trove buried on a website or in a desk drawer?

Would you like another example?

Did you know that the outrageously popular book *Sh*t My Dad Says* started from a Twitter stream?

Moving back to his parents' house after a disastrous relationship, Justin Halpern started Tweeting about the ridiculous things his father said, things that would have otherwise driven poor Justin to drink. These Tweets quickly drew the attention of a huge fan base, followed shortly thereafter by a major publishing house eager to buy a spinoff book.

When he sat down to write this book, Justin took one of his Tweets—*i.e.* The worst thing you can be is a liar…Okay, fine, yes, the worst thing you can be is a Nazi, but then number two is a liar. Nazi one, liar two—and used it as a jumping off point to tell a story about his dad and his childhood. He used these quotes as a vehicle, a way of moving his readers from one incident to the next, to allow insight into not only Justin's quirky father, but also this thing called life.

Do you have some interesting Tweets you could use as writing prompts? Could those 140 characters inspire an essay, or a chapter?

Perhaps you have other content that you could use as starter material:

- Letters
- Facebook posts
- Speeches
- Workshop handouts
- Interviews
- Journal entries
- Presentations

Like Walt's blog posts, or Justin Halpern's Tweets, these might make for some great jumping off points, that little somethin'-somethin' that gets the ball rolling.

I won't delve into each one, because neither one of us has all day, but let's talk about a couple of these categories for a moment to drive the idea home.

Letters

For those of you old enough to remember what one is, to have some stuffed away in a shoebox on some upper shelf, letters can be a wonderful source of starting material.

It's wise to recognize, however, that even the finest, most fascinating letters are often filled with mundane information. You'll have to sift through the inanities—the laundry washed, the runny noses wiped, the sales at Costco—in order to find the gold. Search for the sentences, ideas, images that make for a good story. That outrageous thing a husband said in the heat of the argument. The present sent from Turkey with that dead sister's name sewn into it. The broken down, rusted X-ray machine with three legs your father used (and described) when he ran a clinic in Africa. Highlight these little nuggets; copy them into a document labeled *My Fabulous Book*. You can come back to them when you're ready to write your stories.

Interviews

With the popularity of podcasts and YouTube, many tech-savvy entrepreneurs have created video interviews to promote their business. I know I have.

If you want a book to establish yourself as an expert, coach, or thought leader, a collection of transcribed interviews may be just the way to go.

I'll caution you here, though. If you think you can transcribe an interview and publish it without much work, you're dead wrong. The spoken word, no matter how interesting to listen to, reads like the musings of a schizophrenic on paper. How we communicate verbally is not how we communicate on the page. Lots of editing and shaping is required for clarity.

Transcripts, however, make for a lovely shitty first draft, and that's precisely what we're after right now.

As a side bar, interview questions also make wonderful writing prompts, particularly if you're writing a book with an inspirational message; ditto if you're contemplating a memoir. (More on prompts in the next chapter.) Think about it. How would you answer these questions?

- What are your passions? How did you discover them?

- What's the last thing you did that gave you a real sense of achievement?

- Who are your role models and why?

- What experiences defined the person that you are today?

- Might the answers to these questions be part of your expert positioning story?

NOTE:

If you wish to position yourself as an expert in a given field, then your expert positioning story is critical to your book. The idea is to tell a consistent story about who you are, why your message is important, and what unique expertise you bring to your market. This story connects you to your audience, establishes authority, inspires hope, and motivates action. This story would appear, as mine did here, within the first two chapters of your book.

How do you accomplish all that with a single story? Start by sharing your struggle to succeed, allowing people to relate to you. Then describe your sources of knowledge to demonstrate why you know more than the average bear (certifications, degrees, years of experience, firsthand trial-and-error, etc.). Finally, share your personal stories of success as well as the stories of your successful clients and customers.

If you're not sure how to begin, take a look at how you describe yourself in the About Me section of your website, provided, of course, you have a website. If you give presentations or speeches, how do you prefer to be introduced? Do you have a script you hand moderators? You'll want to rob from these sources

Laying It All Out

It's time to get serious and organize your starting material, to harvest what's usable for your project, and toss what's not. Sometimes we underestimate what we've got; other times we discover that we've got far more fluff than workable clay. Don't shy away from this reality check. You can't fix what you don't face.

Gather the content you already have and put the assorted pieces into one big pile. Print out the blog posts. Type up, or print off your Tweets and Facebook posts. Pull out speeches or workshop materials from the bottom drawer. Track down letters from that bygone era.

Once you've exhausted your desk, attic, bedroom closets, and hard drive, begin sifting through your papers. Look for bits of gold—things that inspire, or support an argument, or add punch to the story you aim to tell.

As you rifle through, type the best quotes, the most interesting lines from that article (or cut and paste them) into your computer. Remember, you've already created a document for it called *My Fabulous Book*. Capture one sentence, one paragraph at a time. When you come across another unrelated, random idea, make a space in your document, then type it below. Nothing needs to fit together right now. Interesting idea. Space. Interesting idea. Space. You're creating sound bites; that's all. You can expound upon them individually later on.

If you're planning on turning your many blog posts, or workshop materials, into a book, begin by looking for common themes in your body of work. Do you have, for instance, five posts about your ability to communicate with cats? Another three about how to find the perfect mate? Separate similar posts into folders, first on your work surface, then into your computer. Write down what you think the themes are on the folders: cats, say, or love. Which is the biggest pile? Which has the most fleshed out ideas? Are there simple sentences that stand out as possible chapter headings?

Push aside the posts that have no identifiable or relevant theme. Before you turn your back on them, are there any good sentences you can save and add to another post, or drop in *My Fabulous Book*?

Good. You're on a roll.

CHEW ON THIS

1. During your scheduled writing block time, gather any material that's useful for your project.

2. Look for common themes and create separate piles for them.

3. Copy these tidbits of material into a Word document labeled *My Fabulous Book*.

4. Browse through blogs on the Internet. Is it time to start your own, as a way of consolidating your message and creating an audience?

STEP TWO

CREATING A SHITTY FIRST DRAFT

CHAPTER FIVE

The Dreaded Blank Page

That's just hunky dory, you say, but what if you have no materials—no old love letters, or pithy Tweets, or blog posts—lying around? What if you're sitting at your desk staring at a blank page, a horrible, merciless blank page? What's worse, this blank page is the first in a long series of blank pages. *This* blank page is the start of your bestselling book.

Tut-tut. Never you fear. This section is all about creating content, either from scratch, or from the sound bites you've managed to gather.

Now this first chapter is a short one, but it's important. I think it best to slay this dragon before we move ahead. Because, regardless of the amount of readymade material you're starting with, there will be days you face that ugly blank page.

Remember those interview questions I mentioned in the last chapter, the ones I told you would make great writing prompts? Well, I'll often use this type of question to help me free write when I don't know where or how to begin my day's work.

A writing prompt is a sentence designed to open the creative floodgates. Sometimes an image, or a picture, can serve to get the juices flowing, too. Get something down on the page, anything, and more words are guaranteed to follow. That's the purpose of the thing.

The idea, when using a prompt, is to write non-stop for ten minutes in response to a statement or question without worrying about spelling, punctuation, or grammar. After you copy the prompt at the top of your page, then set the timer for ten minutes, you'll give your pen (and your mind) free reign to go wherever it wants to go. Your job during this exercise is to let go of the notion that you have to be witty, or efficient. When you free your subconscious from these constraints, out pops long lost memories, interesting images, and other snippets you wouldn't normally have access to.

Raw beginners are not the only ones to benefit from writing prompts. Even if you're one of the lucky few blessed with mountains of starter material and an MFA from the University of Iowa, there will be days when nothing flows. You'll feel mired in the mud.

Writer's block, as this experience is frequently called, can be caused by several things. Often a writer is trying too hard to stay linear—this happened first, then this, then this, or is it the other way around. Other times, the writer is simply guilty of editing in the field—deciding that something isn't worth writing about, even before he gets the first word down. Sometimes writers feel stymied because they're afraid to tell the truth, to hurt or anger someone they love with their words. (More on this bugaboo later.)

Writers, like musicians and athletes, need a workout when they feel stuck. A prompt can focus the mind, renew confidence, and get the words flowing before the writer turns to a project. This is also an excellent way to train your bad self to compose during writing time, not get up and make beef stew.

You can find prompts in all sorts of places:

- Use an interesting Tweet
- Use a catchy line in a book you're reading
- Use a quote.
- Answer a ridiculous question

- Begin with the phrase: I don't ever want people to know....

- Or, I am most afraid of...

- Take a simple sentence (how about one from *My Fabulous Book*) and expand on it: Growth requires pain. Well, tell me about that. How do you know? What's your experience?

Would you like to experiment? The correct answer is yes.

AN ASSIGNMENT FROM YOUR COACH

Choose one of the following prompts, or one from above, set a timer for ten minutes, and write. Don't think, certainly don't edit! Write everything that comes to mind, no matter how odd. Even if you start writing about Uncle Ali's car from 1969. Don't try to write well: Quiet the part of your brain that wants to edit and just go for it. Don't stop until the bell rings.

- Describe the first thirty minutes of your morning. Record all of your sensory impressions. Were you dreaming when you woke up? What were you feeling: fear, dread, elation? What sounds greeted you: voices, radio, birds, or machines? What did you touch and how did it feel: cold, soft, or stubbly? Tastes: coffee, toothpaste, or margarine? How did you feel? What did you see?

- What particular place comes to mind when you think of a strong sense of smell, taste, touch, sound, or sight? Focus on only one of the senses. Perhaps your own bed, or a hospital room, or your grandfather's cow barn, or the brilliant hues at a market stall in Peru. Put yourself there; be fully in that place.

- Write a list of the things in your father's desk drawer.

- Look inside your lunch box or bag in elementary school. What did you see, smell, taste, and touch?

- After you finish your prompt, you may have one or two lines, or a whole new idea from which to continue your writing that day. You'll be surprised what shows up on your page by building on that thought.

- Want another good writing prompt? Check out Amazon.com. They've got tons of books devoted to this topic. Order one. Use it.

CHEW ON THIS

1. Create a list of writing prompts—ten to twenty of them—that you can turn to when you have no clue where to begin. Keep these in your story notebook.

2. This week, begin your block times with a 10-minute writing prompt of your choosing. If you're working in non-fiction, write from your perspective about a particular memory. If you're creating fiction, write from the perspective of one of your main characters, even if you don't know him or her very well yet.

3. Check out Amazon.com for writing prompt books. Order one. Play with it.

CHAPTER SIX

One Brick At A Time

Writing a book involves the creation of one small chunk of material at a time, because to contemplate the project in its entirety is, as I've said, a set up for insanity and failure. Thus the elephant-eating metaphor.

Just because I can, I'm going to switch over to a different metaphor to better illustrate my next few points. Even if you aren't a mason, I'd like you to consider your book as though it were a brick house. Brick houses have different shapes and structures, just like books, but what they all have in common is bricks and mortar. You can't build a brick house without a generous supply of bricks; no matter how gifted you are with a buttering trowel. The same goes for building books, minus the buttering trowel, of course.

The next step you'll need to take—ignoring all of the rest that lie ahead—is to form a single, tiny brick of material. What do I mean by brick? Depending on the genre you've chosen, I'm talking about one of the following:

- One blog post

- One scene
- One expanded, supported idea
- One case study
- One animal photo with a bubble over the head

After all, only after you have enough of these bricks can you build a chapter, then a section, then a book.

Now, what all of these bricks need to contain, to a lesser or greater degree, is a story. We certainly expect that from a novel or memoir, but what about other genres? Well, have you ever picked up an inspirational book, or a how-to, and found yourself, within the first five minutes, bored to tears? Maybe the author made some great points or interesting statements, but the whole thing read like a dry textbook. Want to know the fatal flaw? Easy. It lacked stories.

Here's the thing: Readers gets lost without the supporting story. If you make an important point, you've got to support it with a story or you'll lose your reader. He or she will drop your book, wander off to the café, and order coffee.

Readers crave story, with faces they can attach to, and sensory details. According to scientific studies, our brains light up like the fourth of July when we read about smells, sounds, tastes, touch, and sights. It's what our minds want. It's the details that keep us grounded and wanting more.

If your book falls flat, invariably it's missing stories.

How To Write A Simple Story

I'm going to walk you through my story writing process, and model it for you. I'll explain how I come up with an idea for a story, then how I construct the thing. I'll be composing a scene for my memoir, but you'll want to follow along even if you're writing a case study or a blog. I'll get to genre modifications later.

It's Tuesday morning, my scheduled writing block time, and I'm staring at an ugly blank page. After I get my tea, Mint, and pick at my fingernail polish, Stardust Pink, I'm going to browse through my story notebook. I know what I'm looking for because one idea I wrote down a while back has been swirling around in my head. I've started thinking about it lately, without being consciously aware that I'm doing so.

Here are a few notes I jotted down around that time in my notebook:

1. I heard that song in a restaurant: *I'll Take You Home Again Kathleen*. It made me want to run away. It was the song Dad loved to play on his violin. Why did a Norwegian farm boy from North Dakota obsess about such a sad Irish tune?

2. From *The New York Times Magazine*. A quote from Kacye, a country western singer. "My idea is to push buttons first, scare off the people who are gonna be scared off and then the right people will like you for who you really are."

3. Had a conversation with a friend. About how I was over-reacting to my husband. How I felt like I was being held hostage when he took too long to answer my question. Told her my ex-husband used to take ten hours to answer a simple question. That he liked me hanging on every word. That he would get pissed off if I walked away mid-speech. My friend asked, "Did anybody else ever make you feel like you were being held hostage?" And I remembered my dad. Oh, did I remember my dad. How he would wake me up in the middle of the night to wash the dishes so he could rant about his miserable life.

There it is, that hostage expression I've been mulling over. That's a weird thing to say, though I think it explains a lot about me. I can think of lots of times I've felt this kind of trapped. I can think of lots of times I've written about these moments. I'm pretty sure, however, that I left the broad statement "I felt trapped" dangling there on the page. I'm sure I never bothered to flesh it out in a scene to explain the feeling. What does that mean? Where does my strong reaction come from?

This expression reminds me of a story: My dad dragging me

into the kitchen in the middle of the night. I'm going to dramatize this moment in order to explore the idea of being held hostage. I don't know exactly where it will fit in my larger project, but what the hell.

Here's my broad statement: Sometimes, for no obvious reason, I feel trapped. Like I'm being held hostage. I'm going to type this at the top of my blank page as a sort of writing prompt.

It's time to sketch out this story. Here's the path I'll follow:

I'm going to place my ten-year-old self in the kitchen with my father.

I could bring my mother and brother into the story, but I don't want to complicate things. I'm going to leave them sleeping in their beds.

I'm going to set our story in the kitchen. Dad will have already pulled me out of bed. I want my readers to be in that kitchen with me.

I'm going to illustrate everything that I see. Because my readers want to see what I do. I'm going to describe the stack of dirty dishes on the counter, the open cabinet door above the sink, the one I always bump my head on. The tub of Country Crock margarine with the toast crumbs swirled on the surface that sits over by the refrigerator, and the yellow plastic dishpan in the sink. I'm going to give you a glimpse of my pajama sleeve as it soaks up dishwater; and my dad's short-sleeved, white dress shirt, an intermittent flash in my peripheral vision.

Then I'm going to mention what I smell, because readers want to smell what I do. I'm going to note the whiskey on my father's breath, and the smell of three-hour-old spaghetti sauce on the stovetop, and the grease from the frying pan, and the sweet stench of the guinea pig cage that's sitting on a stool in the corner.

I'm going to describe what I hear. The ticking of the ceramic clock my mom painted in class. The hum of the refrigerator, and the creak of the bedroom door—my brother's—because he wants to keep an ear open in case the evening escalates.

So, here we are—Dad and me—in this kitchen. You, the reader, are in the kitchen, too. You can see, hear, and smell what I do.

You can even feel the grease in the lukewarm dishwater, where my shaking hands are. You can feel the sharp knife I cut myself on because I don't know it's there at the bottom of the pan.

Now I need to paint what it feels like to be ten, pulled from my bed and ordered to wash dishes while my combative father looks on. What it feels like to be trapped in the kitchen with no easy way out. Because to leave means to bring something really bad—what is it? I'm not sure—down on my head. I need to show you, my reader, what it feels like to be trapped by an angry, frustrated, heartbroken man who needs to get the pain off his chest when he doesn't know who else to talk to. Who chooses a child instead of his wife because she's already shut him out and will only make him feel worse.

How do I do that?

My first draft will be shitty; first drafts always are. This child will be an innocent victim. The father will be a monster. I'm going to be OK with that for now because this story is seen through the eyes of a child who has no real understanding of the world. The piece will soften up during revision. Right now, I want to get the situation down on paper. I want to capture a feeling. I want my reader to understand and feel trapped, too.

What will my father say to get the action rolling? We need dialogue. We need to hear his voice. "Do you think it's fair that I work all goddamned day, then I have to come home and wash the dishes too at 10:30 at night?" Maybe that's not exactly what he said—after all, this is forty years ago—but that's pretty close. That's how he sounded. That's about the right feel, the right impact.

And this little girl is going to say something to calm him down. To make herself small, so he won't take out his rage on her. "I'm sorry. I didn't know there were dishes in the sink."

I'm going to have a dialogue going, but I'm also going to mention the actions and the body language of our two characters. I'm going to show you how my father sat at the edge of a worn-out stool; his glassy and unfocused eyes; the clenched jaw; the way his hands shook; how he smoothed that patch of salt and pepper hair over his bald spot. Dad is going to get up, pace, scoop the guinea pig from its cage, pace some more, sit back down. I'm going to focus on him, primarily, because we're seeing this moment through my ten-year-old eyes. We're seeing this through my point of view.

I'm going to build the tension because readers crave tension. I'll show you how Dad jumped up from the stool, as if he were ready to collar me by my pajamas and throw me out into the cold; then, just as quickly, how he controlled his inexplicable rage by pacing that unswept floor; and by sitting back down and stroking that guinea pig on his lap instead.

I'll let you hear how he changes the subject from the goddamned dishes, to his horrible boss at work, who took all the credit for his airplane engine part design. I'll let you hear my interior dialogue, what I'm saying to myself, what I'm thinking. *Can I leave yet? Is he calm enough for me to go back to bed? Or is it too early? Will I bring his fury down on my head?*

After two or three pages, I'll have shown you, my reader, what being trapped looks smells, sounds, and feels like, maybe even tastes like, if I can capture that sense as well. Then I'm going to end my story. I'm going to leave these two people in the kitchen without any sort of resolution because I'm after the feeling—trapped, held hostage—not a clean conclusion.

The Elements Of Story

The basic elements of story are traditionally considered to be plot, character, conflict, theme, and setting.

Right now, however, I want to set aside some of the more abstract elements of story—namely theme and conflict—and focus on the concrete because, if you can identify these elements on the page, you can model them. You'll notice that I add a few of my own.

What do we have in the story I created about my dad and me that merit pointing out and expounding upon?

• **Characters**. I have two: ten-year-old me, and my dad. At this stage of the game I've focused on their physical description. I've shown you Dad's short-sleeved white shirt, his bald spot, and my wet pajamas. I could illustrate a lot more, but I've focused on the most important details—relative to my goal—which emphasize, I hope, what trapped feels like. I'll probably have to play around with them some more.

• **Setting**. We have a kitchen, a messy suburban kitchen, with all of its mundane objects and a few unique things—like the guinea pig cage—thrown into the mix. Did you notice how that cage stuck in your mind? Remember, readers latch on to unusual objects because they often tell a story of their own.

• **Plot**. We've got some action, here. A young girl has been dragged from her bed. She's washing the dishes. She's cleaning the kitchen. The father is ranting, pacing, getting up then sitting back down, and petting the guinea pig. Our characters need to be doing something; they can't be talking heads.

• **Dialogue**. Characters need to speak to each other; they also need to think in sentence form, which is called inner dialogue. The conversations—both external and internal—will often be non-linear, the way they are when we speak in real life. One will ask a question, the other will answer indirectly, maybe even switch the subject. Dad says, "I can't stand my boss, that goddamned Harvey Weiner." The little girl replies, "Can I go change? My pajamas got wet."

• **Body language**. How the bodies of our characters move says so much. Body language gives the reader clues about what emotions the characters are experiencing. Body language also reveals personality; it rounds out the character and makes him or her more relatable to the reader. Look at Dad's eyes, the nervous way he swipes his hair across his head, the shaking fingers, the hunched over shoulders. What does that tell you about him? When writing a certain emotion, think about your body and what happens to it when you're feeling that way. What does it look like from the outside, what does it feel like on the inside?

AN ASSIGNMENT FROM YOUR COACH

Remember how you were supposed to gather material you had lying around the house and type the best bits into a Word document? This document, *My Fabulous Book*, was to be composed of images, ideas, words that you wanted to capture, perhaps paragraphs you grabbed from your resources. Right, you remember now, now that I'm pressuring you. Well, here are some questions I'd like you to consider while you skim the document once again:

- What do you have that would constitute a setting?

- Are there any major characters emerging?

- Do you have bits of dialogue?

- Body language?

- What are some of the plot points?

- What kind of movement, action, activities have you described?

- Which of these story elements seem to be the most fleshed out?

- What sentence, or broad idea, or character, or object inspires you to begin a story?

Do see where you can get a toehold? You see where you might need to focus more intently as you carry on? Good.

Which leads us to your next assignment, because we're cooking with heat now.

AN ASSIGNMENT FROM YOUR COACH

Write a story. Take one of your ideas or paragraphs—either from your newly created Word document or your story notebook—and sketch out a scene. You'll use all of the elements of story we discussed:

- Setting

- Character

- Plot

- Dialogue

- Body language

- Add sensory details to your story—at least one of each kind:

- Sight—what you see, objects, light and dark

- Hear—tone of voice, footsteps, mechanical sounds

- Smell—onions, dish soap, trouble in the air

- Touch—hot, cold, furry, ridged

- Taste—metal, blood, hot chocolate, smoked salmon

Let us be there in that space with you, or your character. It doesn't matter how you end the story. Just begin it. Paint the scene, then leave us hanging at the end. Or not.

CHEW ON THIS

1. Identify the smallest building block you're going to create, based on your genre. Are we talking blog post? Scene? Case study?

2. Identify the elements of story in your Word document, *My Fabulous Book*. What do you have in spades? What is glaringly absent?

3. Make a list of three stories you'd like to flesh out.

4. Choose one and work on it during block time.

CHAPTER SEVEN

Same Story, Different Genre

You'll be creating your own stories, unless you want to get into trouble for using mine, so you'll need to know how to modify them to fit your chosen genre. It bears mentioning that different genres have different requirements. A how-to, for instance, can't be clogged by extraneous details. We don't want Scarlet O'Hara at the top of the spiral staircase when we're trying to understand how to hammer in a nail. Forget the character or the setting in a short story, on the other hand, and you've got yourself a bloody mess.

Just for a moment, let's tweak the story I created about my dad and me and drop it into an assortment of genres (or, more accurately, a genre's building block). I'll spell out the requirements of these chosen genres, so if yours isn't mentioned, you should be able to extrapolate.

Memoir

Unlike autobiographers, memoirists don't want to recount life to death events; they want to focus on a life-changing chapter in their life, or in the life of someone close to them. We're talking about a very specific, narrowed time frame.

When I began my memoir, for instance, I chose to explore the five years I spent living in Iran. I was in my twenties at the time, so a story that takes place when I was ten years old would appear to have no place in the book; the timing wouldn't fit. Every good memoir, however, requires backstory to support and shed light on the current action. Therefore, I might place this childhood story in or around a scene in which I'm locked in a bedroom after a marital fight. A veritable hostage, I certainly would be feeling trapped. How much more powerful would that "current" scene be in light of this window into my childhood, how much more comprehensible, and emotional? I can hardly wait to add it in.

Personal Essay

In a personal essay, which may or may not be part of a collection, the writer writes about an experience without necessarily having to prove a point. The author needs only to introduce the subject and theme (which is an idea that recurs in or pervades the work). This type of essay, as opposed to an academic essay, is based on feeling, emotion, personal opinion, and personal experience.

Remember my motivation to write this story? I wanted a way of exploring what it feels like to be trapped. Perhaps this kitchen scene could be the entry point of an essay in which I build upon that trapped theme. I could follow this story with that locked-in-the-bedroom incident involving my former husband; that would certainly support the theme. Or maybe I could switch gears entirely by attaching a different story about my father. Perhaps I'll lose the trapped theme and discover that the heart of the story is about desperation and loneliness. Who knows where this piece might go?

Short Story

I've lifted this incident from my life, but because I'm worried about my father rolling over in his grave, I'm going to use this scene as a jumping off point from which to tell a different, more inventive story. I'm going to turn this into fiction, a short story, part of a collection held together by some sort of thread. Maybe I'll call the ten-year-old girl Grace; I've always liked that name. Unlike me, however, Grace isn't smart enough to play it safe. She's going to ramp up the tension by doing something stupid, like going back to bed before her father is appeased. Maybe I'll bring the brother out of his room and have him throw a curveball. Perhaps he's kept quiet long enough, and this is the chosen moment to confront the family bully. Or maybe I'll switch narrative perspectives by telling the story from my father's point of view. That would be an entirely different tale, wouldn't it? I won't know what the heart of the short story is until I've played around. All I know is that this will be a stand-alone piece, with a beginning, middle, and end, and a sense of conclusion.

Self-Help

People buy self-help books because they're looking for instruction on solving personal problems. They want to understand why their boyfriend dumped them, or why they can't lose that baby weight, or how to spot a sociopath before they hire him. Readers are very invested in solving a particular problem, but even the most motivated sort will stop turning pages the minute an author fails to support broad, erudite statements with stories that dramatize a point. No matter how profound your pronouncements, no matter how relevant and useful they are to your audience, they'll get lost in the shuffle if they're not linked to a face—a person, fictitious or real.

The case study is often the emotional center of self-help books because it allows us a glimpse of someone with issues just like ours, case in point: People often over react when they feel trapped. We're going to give our readers a face to connect to; this time it's Ann's.

Typically, case studies offer a brief history of the subjects in conflict. Therefore, we could use this story I created as part of Ann's background bio: Ann's dad was a mechanical engineer who hated his job. He had no friends and a troubled marriage. He often pulled his kids out of bed to have someone to talk with. His youngest child, ten-year-old Ann, was his usual choice because she was sensitive like he was, and compliant. Their interactions were at the nexus of Ann's impatience.

I'm going to have to cut out most of the sensory details in the story, but I'm going to isolate the most interesting ones and use them for impact. I'm going to move the story along and limit the dialogue. I'm going to focus on Dad's dialogue because it has some punch. We're going to discuss the impact Dad's words had on Ann, how they left their mark on the adult. We still want to see that kitchen, the movements, what's going on, but we're going to summarize. We'll still have characters, setting, dialogue, plot, and perhaps a little body language, only scaled down.

Motivational

Reading motivational books helps us dream. They open up our mind and allow us a look at other peoples' viewpoints, help us realize how uniquely different each of us are. We get to see how others deal with issues—self-confidence, speaking our minds, settling for less than we deserve, finding our paths—which serves to inspire us, to call us to action.

You'll hear me say this time and time again: There's no better way to build content for your motivational book than by writing a weekly blog. Like other building blocks, blogs need a story and a point. Because blog readers typically have an attention span of a gnat, we writers have roughly 750 words to accomplish our task.

Because of the restricted length of a blog post, I'll need to dial back the sensory details of my story. I'll need to choose the most memorable, the hardest hitting details to keep in the piece—the guinea pig cage, my father swiping his hair across his scalp, the knife at the bottom of the dish pan—and toss the rest. I'll need to drive to the heart of the story quickly. No place to go for this little girl. Can't go back to bed or something awful will happen. Then I'll turn this story into something more universal, something every reader can relate to, that feeling of being trapped. A lesson will come out of the story; what, I won't know until I've had the chance to think about it. The lesson, of course, is the point; the second part of the equation.

Are you getting ideas for your own stories? Do you have a sense of how to play with story elements and their balance for your given genre? If not, hold on and I'll come at it from a different angle in the next few chapters with some student examples.

CHEW ON THIS

1. Study the balance of story elements vs. straight information in the book you've chosen to model. Does this book have enough sensory detail for your taste? Too much? Are there enough faces?

2. Focus on one building block. Decide what's missing. How is the balance off, if at all? What would be more satisfying? What sort of details or elements does it incorporate that interest you most? What, if anything, seems to weigh the story down?

3. Determine how much page space this brick takes up? One page? Two? A half?

4. Make some notes in your story notebook: How much detail will your bricks need? Which story elements? How long should your stories be?

CHAPTER EIGHT

But I Don't Want To Write A Story About Your Dad

A couple of times a year, I conduct an online Build a Book Bootcamp. Much of this book's content, the very one you hold in your hands, was born of that six-week program. And even though I'm an amazing writing coach (the best one on the planet, according to my dog, who should know because he eavesdrops on all of my classes), students invariably have had questions. They understand the story about my dad, the important components, and all of the genre iterations, but they're not quite sure how to apply the information to their own projects. Perhaps the following questions are similar to your own. Not that you would have raised your hand, or anything, Smartypants.

Crystal And Her Spiritual/Self-Help Book

"I want to write this book because I have a lot to say and share. I want to allow my thoughts, ideas and insights to flow out of me and come into physical expression. I want something tangible. Rather than just having the experience of speaking, channeling, and providing insights, I want to create a result. Something I can touch and feel and say, 'I created that. I birthed that.' I want to co-create something tangible with the Universe, my Guides, Teachers, and Angels using my Divine Gift of Communication, and Authentic Self-Expression. This book will be a how-to of sorts, and it will position me as an expert and be used for my teaching and marketing. However, I'm not sure how much story I'll need. Help!"

So here's what I said to Crystal:

Readers Want Faces

I want to take you through my thought process, how I'd approach your project, Crystal, what kind of stories I'd begin to develop and why.

This is a spiritual/self-help book, not a novel or a memoir. Knowing that, I'm going to pare down some of the sensory details because my readers will be looking for a different balance of information vs. scene. They don't want a self-help book to read like a novel, but they do want to feel like they're meeting real people, with real thoughts and feelings, in real situations. Readers want faces.

What do I want my readers to experience? Perhaps the sense that they're divine beings with the power to create at will. How am I going to give them that experience? I'm going to show them how others discovered their divinity and power, how their lives were subsequently transformed.

I'm going to take my readers on a journey with a real person, so they can see exactly how it was done. The best way to do this is by focusing on my clients' stories. I can even use my own. These will be my case studies. Because, don't forget, I'm also interested in positioning myself as an expert. If I can show how I helped others uncover these magical gifts, what benefit that provided them, my readers will assume that I can do the same for them. That, my dear, translates into more business.

How might I tell a client's story to best reveal this inner discovery and transformation? Let me paint her "before" and "after" pictures while showing how I bridged that gap.

Let's start with the "before" picture. What did her life look like; what pain was she experiencing because she failed to recognize these natural gifts within? Then let me think about what, specifically, I did or said in order to facilitate her discovery process. Finally, what did the transformation look like for her once she discovered these hidden gifts, once she crossed over to the other side? What changed? What pleasure did it bring her, specifically; what pain did it alleviate? Think in terms of problems and solutions, *i.e.* she had the problem; I provided the solution.

Do you remember how I focused on the word "trapped" when writing my story? How I was curious about where that particular feeling came from? Why it kept repeating itself in my life? Well, we've got lots of interesting words to explore in this project description, too, "authentic" being one of them.

These days, authentic is a word that gets tossed around like a football. But what does it *really* mean? What authentic means to me may or may not be what authentic means to you, or to the guy who picks up my trash on Friday mornings. Why is this word so important? I'd be thinking about my own struggle with authenticity. Maybe I'd think back to a particular moment in time, a moment when I suddenly realized that being a fake was costing me big time, a moment in time when it was far more painful to pretend to be someone I was not than to reveal the real me. Then I'd ask myself the following questions:

1. Where was I?

2. Who was I with?

3. What were we saying?

4. What objects, smells, sights stick out in my mind?

5. What was I experiencing in my body?

Now, to paint that picture, I'm going to allow readers into my world, let them know what that experience looks and feels like through me.

There are probably lots of stories that come to mind for the word "authentic" alone. Know what? I'm going to paint them all—two pages here, one page there—until I have a whole ream of authenticity stories. Because that's what writing a shitty first draft is all about: Having way more material than is necessary. I want lots of great stuff to choose from, or to cut big swaths from in order to support ideas I haven't even thought to write about yet.

One by one, I'm going to take on those other amorphous words—Divine Love, light, truth, and abundance—and do the same damn thing. Because this is the language of my tribe, my audience is likely familiar with these words, but they don't know what these words mean to me, or to my clients. They don't know the stories behind these words…yet. Once they do, they'll not only understand the words differently, they'll understand themselves in a whole new way. They'll know that I understand them, and their pain. They'll want to work with me because we speak the same language and yearn for the same things.

AN ASSIGNMENT FROM YOUR COACH

If you're writing a motivational, spiritual, or self-help book (or a genre along those lines), answer the following questions in your story notebook:

- What words or broad concepts do I need/ want to explore more fully?

- What pain point or problem do I mean to address?

- What is my recommended solution? What are the specific steps that will lead to transformation?

- How will my readers feel when they turn the last page? What will they finally understand?

- Which faces am I going to paint? Who will my readers meet, and why?

Nina And Her Psychological Thriller

"I want to write a novel about the differences between bad and good people. How it is that we understand the difference, but we can't always tell the bad people from the good? The words "bad" and "good" are often defined by culture, different from one society to the next. And why is it that bad people are sometimes actually good underneath, yet we can't spot the distinction?

I'd like to create a character similar to Snape in *Harry Potter* (who ended up supporting Harry Potter, keeping him from getting hurt, while everyone thought he was the bad guy) or the TV character Dexter, who kills murderers and gets away with it.

Anyway, my genre will be fantasy fiction, a novel with a psychological component, and somewhat inspiring. In other words, a psychological thriller. What do I do?"

And here's what I told Nina:

Defy Expectations

How would I begin to create stories for this project? First of all, this is going to be a character driven novel. What happens during the course of the story (the plot) will be based on who this character is by nature—both the good and the bad aspects—and how he reacts to situations put in his path. I'm not going to worry about plot right this minute; I'm just going to sketch out this dubious character.

What makes for an interesting character—particularly in a psychological thriller—is the shades of gray. Think for a moment about Hannibal Lecter of *Silence of the Lambs*, a cannibalistic serial killer who loves classical music and gourmet cooking. Evil at his core, what alarms us most about him is that which defies our expectations: his polished elegance and his sophisticated tastes. I'm going to look to defy expectations to some extent: I'm going to mix black with white.

Let's say I want to create a character considered evil by his society, like Snape. Well, why do people in his society consider him evil? We humans decide if a person is bad or good by what one looks like, what one says, how one thinks, and how one behaves. These are the aspects of character writers are charged with showing in a scene.

To start with, what does he look like? Maybe I'll put him in bloody clothing, or dress him in studded leather, or give him a rebellious silver Mohawk and place a daisy behind his ear. Or maybe I'll put him in a finely pressed suit with a silk tie and polished shoes to give the impression he's someone fierce, or horribly rich, or selfish. Such details are exactly what readers crave. Seeing as we're all guilty of judging people by their appearance, they also serve to explain society's assessment of him.

Once he's dressed, I'm going to put him in a room with others and start a conversation. What does he sound like? How does he act? What's going on inside his head? I'm going to have him say something that could easily be misinterpreted as offensive, or ominous. Maybe he's rude, or indifferent, or arrogant, or a little too clever for his own good. Maybe he looks straight through women when they talk, or licks his lips until they're chapped and red. I'm going to show how his speech affects the person having the conversation with him, or perhaps those within earshot. Do they get nervous, or angry? Do they reach for a crucifix, or a gun?

Right now, in this two-page scene, I'm not going to reveal any of his finer qualities. I'm going to make it clear why he's seen by society the way he is.

Then, just for fun, I'm going to take my character and stick him in a different setting with a different person. I'm going to surprise my reader by showing how good this character is at heart. There are so many things he could do to reverse expectation: rescue a helpless cat stuck in a tree, slip a hundred dollar bill into a panhandler's cup, or help a street vendor fix his hotdog cart. I need to show him doing something that will change the reader's opinion of him.

I also want my character to react, so I have to give him people and situations to react to. I need to invent some obstacles. I need challenges to come at him from all sides, to rain down upon his head like the plagues of Pharaoh, so we know what sort of man we're dealing with. We're all angels when life goes our way; true character is revealed when we hit the potholes. To keep the tension high, I'll continually reverse my reader's expectation. Sometimes my character will respond graciously to a problem; sometimes he'll come unhinged and wreak mayhem. I want my readers to wonder, hey, wait? Is this guy bad or good? I want them to have to read to the very end in order to make a final judgment call. And guess what? So do they.

AN ASSIGNMENT FROM YOUR COACH

If you're writing a novel, or a short story collection, answer the following questions in your story notebook:

- What theme do I mean to explore and why?
- Who is the main character, the protagonist (a.k.a. the hero) of my story?
- Which of my protagonist's characteristics do I want to emphasize and why?
- What are my protagonist's greatest attributes, his/her biggest flaws?
- What does he or she want more than anything?
- Who, or what, is standing in the way?
- How might I defy expectations?

CHEW ON THIS

1. Answer the appropriate set of assigned questions in this chapter.

2. Regardless of genre, make a list of the words or broad concepts you need/want to explore more fully.

3. Make a list of the faces we're going to see the most.

CHAPTER NINE

Built Like A Brick Sh*t House

Remember, just as you can build a house with enough bricks and mortar, you can build a book once you've created enough stories. These stories—be they scenes, or case studies, or blog posts—will eventually be glued together to form chapters. Your chapters will then be arranged to produce a real, live book.

Let's go back for a moment and review how you made that first brick so you can create the next one, and the next one after that. You took an idea, or a broad statement, or an image, or a memory, and you built a story around it. You put in sensory details, you told us what was being said, what you—or someone else—thought about the events at hand. You placed us in a setting, let us watch the action taking place. In other words, you allowed us to be there with you, or that other real or fictionalized person.

The brick you created, however, may seem random at this

point, maybe even unfinished and awkward. Perhaps your story starts suddenly, or has no real ending, which leaves the reader hanging. Maybe you're wondering what you're going to do with something so incomplete. It probably doesn't look very useful from where you're sitting, which, if you're anything like me, leaves you feeling sort of desperate.

You don't know it yet, but you're doing exactly the right thing. Trust me.

Fine, don't trust me. Prove it to yourself. Start by noticing these funny little unfinished stories in the books that you read. Notice what the author is using them for. If you're reading a motivational book, perhaps the author is using one to support a main idea, or to explain a broad statement with more visual and emotional detail. If you're reading a memoir, or a novel, notice if that incomplete story picks up where it left off later in the book. Do little pieces of it keep cropping up? Might it be a sub-plot, meaning a separate narrative that's going on in the background of the main story? Remember, in a novel or a memoir, there are often several story lines weaving in and out that fuse together by the book's end.

Maybe the story you wrote reached a natural conclusion and it's simply time to move on. Create another brick, something related to the one you've just produced, or not. You don't have to worry about which story would logically come next. Unless you adore writer's block, we're not doing this thing in a straight line. Save yourself the grief. Your goal is to create a pile of random bricks, not struggle with what goes where. We'll get to that bridge soon enough.

By the way, don't worry about writing too many stories. Nothing is a waste. If you don't end up using them right away, you can stick them in a special folder we'll call The Spare Brick Pile. Many of these bricks can be used to plug holes later on. Some of the bricks will be left over. You can use them for other projects. So write what moves you. Capture it all.

AN ASSIGNMENT FROM YOUR COACH

I'm going to pose some questions to get you thinking about what you might want to create next. Particularly if you're totally drawing a blank because you haven't been jotting down ideas in your story notebook. (Bad dog!)

I'd like you to read over the story you've just written. What did you think this story was going to be about when you started it? Did the story become something very different?

Choose the bit you feel delivers the biggest impact. What one sentence do you really like and why? Which one makes you feel like the total freaking genius that you are?

Copy that sentence down on the top of a blank piece of paper and write without stopping for ten minutes. This is your writing prompt. Write down everything that comes to mind—no matter how crazy or off topic—and see what comes up.

Do you think that what you've written might add richness to your original story? Do you think it might be the start of another story? Use the new material accordingly.

The Mortar

When the time comes—and you don't need to worry about this while you write your stories—you're going to cement your bricks together with mortar. Just so I don't leave you wondering what the hell I'm talking about, this mortar will include one of, or a combination of the following:

1. **Exposition**—This is when you, the narrator, step out of the scene and summarize what has taken place. In the Old Testament of the Bible, for instance, we learn that the Jews wandered in the dessert for forty years. These forty years are described in a couple of paragraphs. We do not stay with the Jews, sandy step by sandy step, for four long decades. The summary of these years gets us to the real action, where the important stuff starts to happen.

2. **Transitions**—Certain words or phrases can help carry a thought from one sentence to another, from one idea to another, or from one paragraph to another. You likely used transitional words—*i.e.* because, however, or furthermore—when you created your first story.

3. **Devices**—Transitional devices link sentences and paragraphs together smoothly so that there are no nasty jumps between ideas, or points in time. Such devices are particularly useful when you wish to join the main story line to sub-plots or backstory. They work by looking backward and reaching forward, by repeating words and ideas. Here are some ways to do that:

A. **Sensory details**—Follow a sound, or a smell, or a taste back and forth through time and place.

B. **Objects**—A red ball in the present moment trails off into a ball bouncing across the playground yard when the narrator was a child.

C. **Dialogue**—A character is speaking, but we go back in time to what that person used to say, or what someone else once said on that topic (and we immediately understand why that informs what's going on in the present). And, voila, we're back to 1969.

D. **Appearance or setting**—While looking at a man with a mustache on the beach your father suddenly appears.

It's the mustache that reminds you of dear old Dad, or the beach, you're not sure which, but we follow you there anyway.

All that being said, (Do you like this transition I'm employing?) let's not lose track of the job at hand, people. We want bricks, lots and lots of bricks. The mortar doesn't need to be mixed until we finish our shitty first draft. I'm only giving you the 411 so you can see far enough ahead to settle on down.

CHEW ON THIS

1. Create a special folder called The Spare Brick Pile. Put things you cut from your document, or aren't sure about, here

2. Take a powerful line from a story you've written. Use it as a writers' prompt and see what develops.

3. Open a book you're reading, preferable the one you've chosen to model. Pick a random page. Find the story. (*Hint: Look for the face, a specific person being described.) Decide if the story is complete, or if it gets picked up and expounded upon later in the game.

4. On that same page, just for fun, identify the mortar: the material or device used to connect two stories/scenes together.

STEP THREE

DEVELOPING AN OUTLINE

CHAPTER TEN

Order In The Court

Not sure where the stories you've just written are going to go? Feeling dangerously disorganized? No worries. There's no *one* right way to build your book. I repeat: There's no *one* right way to build your book. An individual story, one little brick, could likely be dropped into fifteen different places throughout your manuscript. More importantly, by the time you complete your last draft, the one that you'll publish, you'll have moved most of your stories around a dozen times anyway.

Possibilities are great, but for those of you who get a little squirrely without a set plan, we're going to create some structure to keep you cool and composed. We're going to create a blueprint for your book. That way, when you're looking at the magnificent collection of bricks at your feet, bricks you've created one by one, you'll have some idea what to do with them all. You'll know how to organize and connect these seemingly disparate stories so they come out whole. As Steve Chandler says in his book *Shift Your Mind*, "Energy is robbed by indecision. Not knowing what to do next, trying so hard to decide which course to take, it wears you out." A blueprint will minimize uncertainty and buttress your confidence.

This blueprint, by the way, is your Table of Contents. The Table of Contents is that page at the very beginning of a book—most books have them, but some don't—that lists the chapter titles and the page numbers on which they begin.

So, take out the book that you bought; the one you thought would serve as a good model. If you completely disregarded that assignment, Lone Ranger that you are, choose a book that you have lying around. Found the Table of Contents yet? Good, because I'm going to model how to use it to create a detailed plan for your own book.

For those mavericks who like figuring out things as you go along, who don't need a damn blueprint to keep you on track, you'll want to create a Table of Contents anyway. Your Table of Contents tells readers not only about the topic of your book and its scope, but your approach to the subject and tone. I'll give you an example. I was browsing through a bookstore in D.C. a while back when I ran into an interesting little book. It was called *China in Ten Words*. The Table of Contents had me at hello. Here's what it looked like in all of its glorious simplicity:

People
Leader
Reading
Writing
LuXun (Must have no good translation in English)
Revolution
Disparity
Grassroots
Copycat
Bamboozle

Some of the words, like Bamboozle, made me want to buy the book just to see what the author would write about. When I leafed through the introduction, here's what the author told me: "My goal, then, is to compress the endless chatter of China today into ten simple words; to bring together observation, analysis, and personal anecdote in a narrative that roams freely across time and space; and finally to clear a path through the social complexities and staggering contrast of contemporary China."

If you're scratching your head searching for the perfect ten words to describe your book's content, don't worry; simple is actually harder than it looks.

Nevertheless, we're going to break this blueprint concept down in the next couple of chapters using student examples.

> **NOTE:**
> Pay attention to how I'm structuring this next section if you're writing an instructional book. Your readers can take in only so much information at any given time. You won't want to stick too many bricks together in one go, even if they're related. You'll want to find ways to create short and sweet chapters, which allow for a breather. After all, you don't want your readers flooding the mental health hotlines, or do you?

If you're writing a quote book about your clairvoyant Chihuahua, feel free to skip ahead. I mean, really, how tough can that be?

CHEW ON THIS

1. Locate the Table of Contents in the book you chose to model.

2. List ten or more words you might use to describe the content of your book, words that you might use in a chapter title.

3. Throw your stories up in the air and let them settle where they may. Just kidding.

CHAPTER ELEVEN

Tuesdays With Maggie

Have you chosen to write a memoir? Even though I *tried* to scare you off?

Well, listen up; this chapter is just for you. If you're writing a novel, or even a motivational book, you'll find some excellent points here, too.

One of my students—I'll call her Maggie—decided that she wanted to write a book like *Tuesdays with Morrie*. Confident in her writing skills, she felt ready to take on an involved memoir. More than anything, she yearned to tell the story of her mentors and how they influenced the woman she's become. Using this example, let's get to work on creating a blueprint for Maggie. I'll show you, step by step, how I analyze both the Table of Contents and the book itself.

According to the cover of *Tuesdays with Morrie*, this memoir is about an old man, a young man, and life's greatest lesson. Published in 1997, it was enormously popular in the States. I remember it well; perhaps you do too. It had heart.

Opening up the Table of Contents, I see a list of twenty-seven chapters. Wow, that's a lot. Many of these chapters, however, are very short, only one or two pages long. The others are seven pages or so. That gives me a feel for the book's structure. Short chapters offer a quick read, which folks in our busy culture seem to like.

Here are some of the chapter titles: *The Curriculum, The Syllabus, The Student.* These are all academic words. They remind me of my university experience. So there's a theme afoot. I'm going to expect a tale about a college-style relationship, one involving higher learning.

When I scan further down the Table of Contents, I find a different type of chapter title: *The 1st Tuesday.* This has a subtitle as well, which serves as a description: *We Talk About The World.*

This chapter is followed by *The 2nd Tuesday: We Talk About Feeling Sorry For Yourself.*

We get all the way to *The Fourteenth Tuesday: We Say Good-Bye.* Then we have *Conclusion.*

Well, I know what I'll be getting from this book. The lessons are clearly spelled out in the sub-titles.

Notice the structure: point, then supporting story. This is really important, particularly if you're writing a motivational book. You don't tell a story without a point. You don't make a point without a supporting story.

Analyzing Chapter Content

If I were Maggie, who, if you remember, is using this book as her model, I would take a closer look at these chapters to see what they're composed of. Maybe there are lots of quotes, or bullet points, or tons of dialogue. Maybe each chapter begins with a recipe for chip dip. (Believe me, I've read stranger.)

The first chapter seems to be little more than a single page. It's an introduction, telling us in simple, yet emotional terms what this story is about. Nothing fancy. There's a little page break that looks like a squiggle, or a set of squares, which serves to transport the reader from the present moment back in time. We then get another page and a half of backstory where we witness the young man—the author—graduating from college, then introducing his parents to the old man—Morrie. The old man is his professor, and he's crying. Crying because the relationship between the two of them means something to him—something beyond what one would expect. This backstory is in italics. This is how the author has chosen to clarify the time jump.

The first few chapters are designed to bring the reader into the story. To give us the faces. They also answer the all-important questions:

1. Who do we have here?

2. Why should I care about these people?

3. How do they feel about each other?

4. What's at stake for them, meaning, what do they stand to lose?

5. Why should I want to know more about them, and their situation?

Again, if I were Maggie, I'd go through the subsequent chapters and look for patterns. How long are the chapters and what are they composed of?

Let's jump to *The 4th Tuesday: We Talk About Death*. Right away we start with a story: The two men are talking to each other in a home office. The lesson about dying is right up front in the dialogue. "Let's begin with this idea," Morrie said. "Everyone knows they're going to die, but nobody believes it." The lesson is in the dialogue because we're dealing with a memoir, not a motivational book where readers expect the lesson to be spelled out and set apart in an obvious way, then supported by a relevant story. In creative non-fiction and fiction, we need the lessons to be tucked into the story. They can't be too obvious, or the author scores a D- for being pedantic.

What else do we have in this chapter, besides this conversation between the two men? We see the backyard through the window, which places us even deeper in the setting. We get some details about what's going on in Detroit, where the young man is living, which ground us in that particular era. We're given snippets of each man's current life and philosophy and personal history in between the lines of this conversation; which, as promised by the chapter title, resembles a truly powerful college lecture.

Having flipped through the remaining chapters, here is what this book is: a collection of stories about death, about what someone who is dying can teach us about living. Spelled out in twenty-seven short chapters are the lessons and the story of the relationship, which is the emotional heart of the book. We care about the message because we care about the faces.

Now, you might ask, what the hell is Maggie supposed to do with this analysis? Maybe you don't care about Maggie, being selfish and all, but surely you'd like to know how all of this applies to you.

Maggie is going to sketch a blueprint for her book.

Instructions For Maggie's Blueprint

1. Break out a piece of paper and number one through sixteen from top to bottom, which will represent the chapters. Why not one through twenty-seven, the total number of chapters in *Tuesdays With Morrie*, you ask? That may be too complicated to start out with, so I'm giving her (read you) a short cut.

2. The first Chapter will be the introduction. Mitch Albom, author of *Tuesdays With Morrie*, chose to break apart his introduction into five short chapters. For the sake of simplicity, Maggie is going to do it in just one. Like Mitch did, here are the questions Maggie needs to answer in her intro: Who are these people and what is this story about? Readers need to know this or they won't press on.

3. Chapters two through fifteen will be a list of lessons Maggie will have her characters/mentors teach us. If Maggie doesn't know why she's writing about these people, what they taught her, what their fourteen lessons were, well, she's going to have to stop dead in her tracks and do some soul searching. Because, in order to fashion those powerful supporting stories, those bricks, she's going to need the points. Otherwise she's going to get way off track and end up in Bangladesh instead of Buffalo.

4. Chapter sixteen will be the conclusion. In the end, when all is said and done, what does Maggie make of all of these lessons? What does she now understand about life that she didn't before? How has this knowledge changed her? Without change, we've got nothing worth writing about, or reading.

CHEW ON THIS

1. Take out the narrative book (novel or memoir...) you chose to model.

2. Examine the length and composition of the chapters. Are they filled with setting description, background information, back and forth dialogue? Do the lessons stand out, or are they tightly woven into the storyline?

3. Make some notes about what you'll need in your chapters to serve as a guideline, either in your story notebook, or in the book itself. We'll get to creating your blueprint soon enough. Patience, Pumpkin.

CHAPTER TWELVE

Sheila On The Edge

Are you a thought leader or an expert? Have you decided to write a book to showcase your unique process for fixing a specific problem? Do you want to inspire people, to offer them your perspective, your hard-won experience, so they can live a better life? Might the lessons that you've learned—never leave a pig unattended in your living room, for instance—save others pain and time? Then this chapter is just for you.

One of my students, Sheila, chose to model my husband's motivational book, *Journeys on the Edge: Living a Life That Matters*. (She's a coach and an expert in her own right, so her choice makes a lot of sense.) I happen to have about three hundred copies lying around the house. I'll go grab one of them.

As I did for Maggie's project, I'm going to show you how I analyze this book and the Table of Contents, so we can create a blueprint for Sheila.

On the back cover of *Journeys* it says, "Squeezed by time and snared in responsibility, so many of us fail to live the lives we once imagined. But there is another way." From this statement one can infer that lessons abound.

> **NOTE:**
> This is a shameless plug for Walt's book.

Peeking at the Table of Contents, I find a list of forty-two chapters. Again, that's a lot of chapters. Makes sense, however, knowing that this book started out as a collection of blog posts.

Some of these chapter titles are provocative, and perhaps a little silly: *The Trouble Newton Caused*; *I've Been Framed*; *Before You Know it, it's Lunchtime*. This tells me that the book is going to have some humor. I'm curious. What could these titles mean? What might the lessons be? When I skim through, I find that each of the chapters is three or so pages long, and ends with a little quote.

Walt's introductory chapter is five pages long and, like *Tuesdays with Morrie*, it tells us what the book is about, who the author is, and why we should care about him and his story. He's setting the stage. We know up front what the struggles will be. Remember, readers want to know what the problem is right away. They don't want to wade through thirty-nine pages, or chapters, to figure that out. Without a problematic situation, or ten, there's no story. Game over. The book gets tossed.

Let's jump ahead to Chapter 12: *The Other F* Word*. What's it made of?

Walt starts with an idea, the F-word. Naughty minxes that we are, we think it means fuck, but he pulls the old bait and switch and tells us he means failure. He takes this broad topic—failure—and tells us a short story about what was expected of him in his family of origin, how he wasn't supposed to fail. This is a pencil sketch without a lot of sensory detail; few story elements save character and dialogue. He follows this story with several quotes about failure from other sources; there are six in all. Then we learn about Walt's friend Bob—this could be a client, or an acquaintance—who has a very different take on the matter. This is an opportunity to consider failure from a different perspective in more depth. Walt wraps the chapter up by giving us a takeaway, a little lesson that he's learned by looking at failure through these other lenses: "If we don't retreat from failure, but learn from it instead, it can catapult us to brilliance." This is his conclusion, his point.

The other chapters seem to follow this formula: broad idea, supporting stories, lesson at the end. Sound familiar? I knew it would.

Heading back to the Table of Contents, I notice that, while there are numerous short chapters, they're organized into five sections. These sections are a framework, which deserve study.

Section One is called *Resuscitating Your Dreams*. It has a sub-title: *Remembering What Rocks Your World*. This would imply that all of those little chapters that are housed in this section are going to have something to do with the broad idea of remembering your dreams. Section Two is called *Eating the Elephant*, and the sub-title, *Taking the First Bite*. (Hmm. Sound familiar?) I figure the associated chapters will be about taking something big, like building a book, breaking it down into manageable steps, then taking on the first one. The other three sections indicate that this is a guidebook of sorts, where the steps necessary for living the life of your dreams are spelled out and supported with relevant stories. To end the book, we have an epilogue, which serves as a conclusion, tying the ideas together into a neat little bundle.

Sound like the kind of book you'd like to write? If you're an expert, a speaker, or a coach, I'm betting the answer is yes.

What do your steps look like? How would you break down your unique process for your reader? What stories do you have to support your recommended line of action?

Just so we're keeping horses in front of carts, know that Walt took his individual blog posts—a whole big pile of them—and moved them around like chess pieces to see which reading order made the most sense. After several configurations, he began to see some common themes in his blogs, which gave him the idea for a structure that would hold them all together. His message— the importance of living the life of your dreams—was born of this structure.

Now, what would I do if I were Sheila, if I wanted to use the structure of *Journeys on the Edge*? Let's break the steps down for Sheila like we did for Maggie using the Table of Contents. Better yet, let's break the steps down for you.

Instructions For Sheila's Blueprint

1. Take out a blank piece of paper and write down the numbers one through seven. These represent the intro chapter, the five major sections, and the epilogue or conclusion, in that order. Leave a lot of space between numbers one through seven because we're going to pencil in a little more structure.

2. Write the word "Introduction" by number one. Beneath that word, list, line by line, the questions that will need to be answered before you move on: What is this story about? Who are you? Why should the reader care?

3. For Section One, which you'll jot down by the number two, type the following: "The most important lesson I've learned (or seen others learn) is _____." As a subset of Section One, write the numbers one through five. These will represent the blog posts or chapters related to this lesson. If you already have a lot of written content, think of this as your organizing drawer. The statement can also serve as a writing prompt if you're starting from scratch, if you haven't been writing a blog for years on end. You'll begin by writing one story (or a thee-page blog post) that supports this lesson, then a different one after that, then another.

4. For Section Two, by which you'll type by, that's right, the number three, write the following: "The second most important lesson I've learned, or seen others learn, is _____." Now do the same exact thing. And do that for each of the following sections, all the way up to Section Five.

5. By number seven, write the word Epilogue, or Conclusion. Then write this question: "What have all of these

things taught me, and why should others care?" The reader wants the author to go back and digest everything, then leave them with the essence. You'll need to summarize, by the way, not only at the end of the book, but at the end of each chapter as well.

Consider this a starting structure. By the time you publish your book, the introduction and conclusion will have been revised multiple times. The sections will have shape shifted because you'll learn that what you thought was the lesson was not really the lesson at all. You're not going to know that, however, until you write the first shitty draft. To get to the final product, you must start. And it's so much easier to start when you can see, in black and white, what you'll need to produce.

CHEW ON THIS

1. Take out the motivational/inspirational book you chose to model.

2. Examine the length and composition of the chapters. Are they filled with quotes, lists, bullet points, song lyrics, pictures of cats? Are the lessons clear? Do the stories support the points?

3. Answer this: How is the unique process broken down for the reader? Is it built into a step-by-step structure the way this book is?

4. Make some notes about what you'll need in your chapters to serve as a guideline, either in your story notebook, or in the book itself. (That's why I told you to buy the thing!)

CHAPTER THIRTEEN

Do It Yourself Blueprint

Ready for a stretch break? Good. Get up and jump around a bit. Touch your toes. Do a few side bends.

Before we get to work on your outline, I'd like you to notice something interesting. Are you feeling antsy or distracted? Are you wondering if you should tromp to the kitchen and forage for leftover birthday cake? Have you checked your smartphone, like, 937 times in the last half hour? Well, that's because you've just read through several chapters of straight information with very little story to ground you. There were no faces you could identify with, or sensory details to latch onto. Iman wasn't crying at the kitchen table; my dad wasn't pacing back and forth; Jane Austin darned no socks. Beware of information overload if you're writing a how-to or a self-help book. In the quest to move things along, to pack it all in, we risk losing our readers to overwhelm.

Did you find the birthday cake? Are you good? OK, get up. This time, fetch that book you chose to model. And while you're at it, grab a few sheets of paper and an old fashioned pencil. You might have to sharpen it. We're gearing up to copy us an outline.

What have we got? Nervous because your chosen book doesn't have chapters, or worse, has 150 mini chapters? Well, never you fear, I'm going to give you something to work with right now.

AN ASSIGNMENT FROM YOUR COACH

On a blank piece of paper write down the numbers one through fifteen in the left hand column. (I like Roman numerals. They make me feel sophisticated, worldly.) By each number, create a chapter title. Easy does it, Precious. These are broad, general idea titles that'll eventually change. You're not etching them in stone.

Leave a lot of space between the numbered chapter titles because we're going to make some notes.

Under each chapter title, write a list of the subject areas that will be covered. What's going on in these chapters? If you're writing a motivational book, a self-help guide, or a how-to, what lesson will you teach us? What case studies are going to appear? Which personal story might support the point?

If you're writing a novel or a memoir, what's the main action taking place? What are the five or so plot points that will drive the story forward, or to a conclusion? Which characters are involved? Where in time and space are they? (If you're not sure what a plot point is, don't worry, I'll spell that out in the next chapter.)

Now that we've got a general idea sketched out for each chapter, let's get a little more specific; dig up some more details. Under the brief chapter description and the list of subjects covered or plot points, write down five to seven questions a reader might ask while following that story. What might they want to learn more about?

Ready for the next step? Take each of those questions and remove the question marks. Turn them into statements.

These statements, five or so for each chapter, are going to be your writing prompts for the next several weeks. Perhaps several statements will be fleshed out in one scene. Perhaps one statement will only require a few lines of explanation. Perhaps the first statement will inspire three pages of scene, the next, a few lines of explanation; another will produce enough material to be a separate chapter. Regardless, you'll have a good feel for what needs to be spelled out, or dramatized, by chapter's end.

Are you seeing the method to this madness?

A Little Visual For The Impaired

Just for this exercise, imagine that you'd like to write a memoir about the decade your family spent living in Uganda. That's a specific chapter in your life, which is good, but it's also a decidedly broad topic. Where do you start? What do you include? What do you leave out? Which incidents are most representative of that era, and which might draw a reader in?

I've taken the liberty of penciling in the who, what, where, and when, then playing what I lovingly refer to as The Question Game in order to create the start of an outline. You're going to do the same exact thing. Here's what I came up with:

I. *My Father Decides To Move Us To Africa*

It's 1971. We begin in Boston, and land in Uganda. The characters include my father, mother, sister, our dog, Rex, and me.

1. My father takes a teaching position at a hospital.

2. We say goodbye to our friends and family.

3. We take a twenty-hour flight and land in the dust.

4. We must find our way to our new home alone.

5. There is no furniture when we arrive.

A. Why did your dad want to go to Uganda of all places?

B. What did you think about the move? Were you scared?

C. What did your father expect when you landed?

D. How different was your new home from the one you left?

E. What did your mother think and say about this change?

a. My dad chose Uganda because of a *National Geographic* article.

b. I thought we were going to meet Tarzan.

c. My father was promised the world, including a car and driver.

d. We lived in a beautiful Victorian and moved to a tarpaper shack.

e. My mother put on an apron and vowed to turn our shack into a home.

II. *Our First Experience In Our New Village*

III. *The Day A Snake Kills Rex*

IV. *My Sister Gets Lost*

V. *Idi Amin Takes Over The Country*

And so on and so forth.

CHEW ON THIS

1. Open the book you have chosen to model and copy the structure of the Table of Contents in outline form on a sheet of paper.

2. If the Table of Contents is too complicated, or non-existent, create a well-spaced, numbered list of 8-15 chapter titles.

3. For each chapter title, write down a very brief description of what it's about.

4. Beneath these descriptions, write a list of the subject areas that will be covered, or the plot points.

5. Beneath these lists, write down five questions your reader will likely ask, then turn these questions into statements.

CHAPTER FOURTEEN

How To Keep Your Reader From Yawning

For those of you who have chosen to write a novel or memoir, genres that require far more time and skill, I'd like to step back for a moment and offer you a little craft lesson on the development of plot points. Think of this as a bonus; like supersizing your fries.

The question at hand is what, specifically, will take place in each chapter?

Remember, your entire book is going to change by the time you complete the final draft. But it's so much easier to write your book when you have an idea of what major events will occur in each chapter. That's why we listed these events in your outline.

Here's the other reason why. In fiction and creative non-fiction, things have to happen in your story. Lots and lots of things. There have to be problems; people have to change the way they view the world; characters must start out one way and end up very different at the end.

As your readers, we need to have a sense of forward movement, or we yawn and close the book. (By the way, characters wandering aimlessly from room to room, or picking at their toenails, does not constitute movement.) A character must be born, injured, in trouble, getting married, changing in some way, understanding something for the very first time, going on a trip, expecting company, something: We just can't have talking heads—two or more characters in conversation—page after page. We need events.

A plot point is a significant event that spins the action around in another direction. Plot points are those obstacles your characters must face. Obstacles can be very subtle—your character suddenly realizes she's forgotten her keys—or very dramatic—someone just busted down the door and is holding everybody hostage with a gun.

I love what Anne Lamott, author of *Bird By Bird*, says about plot: Plot is "what people will up and do in spite of everything that tells them they shouldn't, everything that tells them that they should sit quietly on the couch and practice their Lamaze, or call their therapist, or eat until the urge to do that thing passes."

Have you ever watched a horror movie? Home alone, a young girl hears a noise in the basement. And instead of picking up the phone and dialing 911, she gets up, grabs a flashlight, and goes to investigate. And you start shouting at the screen, "NO, don't do that. You'll be sorry." Well, that inadvisable stuff, that's plot. That inciting incident—the noise in the basement—that's a plot point.

AN ASSIGNMENT FROM YOUR COACH

Pick up the novel or memoir you've chosen to model. Turn to the first or second chapter. In that chapter, identify the plot point(s), the obstacle(s), your protagonist must face and eventually overcome. What, in other words, is the problem?

The Question Game

Let's break this down even further. "Ann," you might say, "I don't know what's going to happen in my first chapter. How the hell am I supposed to know what should happen in my fifth chapter? How do I get this stuff down into an outline?"

Good question. Let's play The Question Game to form an outline:

Chapter One

1. Who are you going to introduce us to?

2. Where do they live?

3. What is their big problem?

4. What is keeping them from living the life of their dreams?

5. Why must things change for them?

6. How are they going to get what they need?

Notice I'm asking who, what, where, how, and when questions.

Let's do the same thing for Chapter Two, then the next, and the next. Let's ask some who, what, where, when and how questions and see what changes. Who are we going to meet? Where are we going? What problems are cropping up unexpectedly?

Allow your imagination to go wild. Have some fun. This is the joy of creative writing. If you're writing fiction, you get to make up some terrific stuff. If you're writing memoir or some other type of creative non-fiction, you get to handpick juicy events from the past, and the perfect details. Notice that I'm not asking you to capture major themes like love, or the problems associated with communism, or man's inhumanity to man at this point. Your job is to create characters who run into problems, which they bounce off of like billiard balls. You are not to wax on, say, about the unfairness of child labor in Victorian England. Your job is to tell the story of some orphan boy who grows up in the poor house, who then gets into trouble because he's hungry and wants another bowl of porridge. We want to read a story about that little boy. We want a face, a specific, well-drawn character we can attach to. Your job, after you've created these faces, is to throw rocks at them so we can see how they deal with it all. So we can root for them, or despise them for their cruelty.

CHEW ON THIS

1. Identify the plot points in one chapter of the book you've chosen to model.

2. Play The Question Game for each chapter of your novel or memoir (or other narrative genre) to create a more substantive book outline.

3. For inspiration, put someone you don't like in a tree, throw rocks at him, and see what he does. Jot his responses down in your story notebook. Just kidding.

STEP FOUR

STAYING STEADY THROUGH THE STORM

CHAPTER FIFTEEN

There Will Be Obstacles, And Blood

I'm going to assume that you've been doing exactly what I've told you to do because you're either compliant, or very keen on finishing your book. If you've been writing up a storm, you've likely run into some obstacles. Everyone does. You may be pacing back and forth, chewing your nails, because you have no idea what to do next. How, pray tell, are you going to push ahead with that glaring problem staring you in the face? Yes, your job right now is to create a shitty first draft. Yes, your job is to create as many bricks—stories—as you can. But some issues feel like show stoppers. When you sit down to write, you actually feel afraid.

Remember when I lifted up the skirt and showed you what the writing process really looks like? I bet you're thinking something is wrong with you, with the way you're doing things, because you've forgotten that a good writer can make it all look so damn easy. Look at Paulo Coelho, the famous Brazilian writer who seems to come out with a new bestseller every frigging year. His sentences are so simple. Consider his first line from *The Alchemist*: "The boy's name was Santiago." Really? Any second grader could come up with that. Duh!

If you were to completely misinterpret what I mean by modeling a book, you might launch your story in a similar way: "The girl's name was Rosemarie." Three sentences in, however, you'd realize that it's not so obvious where to go with Rosemarie, unless, of course, you'd like to risk plagiarizing Coelho. There are simply way too many choices at hand. If you take Rosemarie down one path, you'd have one story, if you take her down another path, it's a different story entirely. Doubt sets in. The minute you solve one problem, another one pops up to take its place.

Welcome to writing. Actually, welcome to life.

Dry your tears, my pet. In this section, we're going to address some of the most common issues and fears that may crop up along the way.

The Trouble With Beavers

But before I begin, I'm going to make a point: When you run into an obstacle, any obstacle, do not run away from it. Don't start in on a different story (or even a different project) thinking it will be easier because you don't immediately know how to solve your problem. Be patient.

Now I'm going to tell you a story: Once upon a time, Walt and I were out for a morning run. It so happens that our running route takes us past a river. Because it was springtime, we began to spot signs of heightened animal activity. The beavers in particular had been very busy.

We trotted past a very large oak. Apparently the beavers had been gnawing on it for weeks on end. They almost had the whole tree down. Another day or so of work, and the trunk would likely snap in half. But then, a little farther down the road, I noticed that the beavers had started in on another tree. They'd done quite a job on it as well. That's when I spotted the rest. I counted all of the partially gnawed trees, and do you know how many there were? Fifteen! And not a single one had been taken down, which, I believe, is the goal of the beaver.

See, a beaver's job, for those of you unfamiliar with the habits of North American wildlife, is to bring trees down into the water in order to construct a damn. They live in small, calm pools of water that are created by these damns. Damns don't miraculously appear because a beaver would like them to; they must be built. That's how nature works.

Being the intuitive sort, I could practically hear what these beavers were thinking. "Damn, I'm tired. I don't know how much longer I've got to chew on this stupid tree." Leaning back on his tail and looking around, one of them must have spied a smaller tree; a tree with deceptively soft bark. "Let's go for that one. That one looks easier to take down. Not as big, not so complicated."

You might not know this but beavers are short and quite near-sighted. They can't step back far enough to see the trees for the forest. They're blind to the fact that, if they just kept at it, if they just worked through the ubiquitous obstacles, that old oak would fall sooner rather than later. Cursed with poor memories as well, beavers are incapable of remembering that the minute they start in on a different tree, they will, as God is their witness, invariably run into the same set of problems they encountered with the first.

Don't be a beaver.

Stick with your big tree and gnaw on it until you take the damn thing down. Your job is to get that tree in the water, not to chew on fifteen different trunks. Trust that, like a nearly blind beaver, you don't have a decent vantage point. You can't tell how long your project is going to take until it's done, and that's OK. Be patient. Keep gnawing. Don't quit and scurry off to work on something that looks easier. Adjust your angle, brush your teeth, whatever, just keep at it.

AN ASSIGNMENT FROM YOUR COACH

It's time to create a title for your book. *My Fabulous Book* is pretty good, but you'll notice that there are a lot of books out there with that very same title. What's the name of your book? Sure, it's going to change by the time you're done, but let's get to know your baby on a first name basis. That way you won't be as tempted to throw it out with the bathwater; to go after something cuter. Need some ideas? Browse the bookstore for catchy titles, or check out List-mania! on Amazon.

Too Much Of A Good Thing

On a related topic, if you're just getting started, having too many story ideas to choose from may not sound like much of a problem. I mean, complaining about your active imagination is not unlike whining about your inability to gain weight. You'd be hard pressed to find people to feel sorry for you, especially me. But what if you have so many ideas, you can't hone in on a clear direction? What do you do when you're all over the place? When you want to write fifteen different stories all at once?

Simple: Pull out your outline.

There's a good reason I asked you to create an outline for yourself. Yes, this outline will likely change by the time your book is done, but for now, it serves as an organizational tool.

There's also a good reason I asked you to use a story notebook. Got a plethora of ideas? Terrific! Write a list of them in your story notebook. *i.e. I want to write about my client, Gertrude. I want to mention her fear of cats and how she's been married twelve times and how she finally learned to meditate and lose 300 pounds.* Write until you can't think of another story idea to write about. Write until you exhaust your mania.

Then go back to your outline. Where might this story about Gertrude fit? Chapter 2, subsection 4: *How To Lose Weight By Meditating*? Maybe it doesn't fit anywhere. Maybe you want to leave that story alone for now. Maybe you'll come back to it later, find an appropriate spot for it after realizing that Gertrude's story is really about surviving divorce with cat therapy. Or maybe you'll stick it in your next book.

Write things down in your story notebook with enough detail so, when you go back to it in two weeks, or two years, you'll remember what the hell you were thinking of. You won't loose anything if you jot notes. That's why you carry the story notebook *everywhere*. You don't have to deal with everything all at once.

And that's why you have an outline. So you can decide which stories to focus on first.

Lose Friends And Alienate People

Writers worry a lot. Worry is what feeds our procrastination; why we'd rather clean that disgusting barbeque grill than sit in front of our nice, clean computers. We worry that we're hacks; that we have nothing new to say on a subject, that we're frittering away our time on yet another project that we're never going to see to completion. However, there's one fear that looms above them all, the granddaddy of the pack: the fear of writing about other people and the trouble that may cause.

For professionals writing self-help books, such dread often arises in the form of this question: What should I do if I write about real people, without their permission? If I discuss clients and patients, wouldn't I betray their confidence?

Here's the scoop: As writers we want to stick to the truth as closely as possible, unless of course we're writing fiction, but we can slap a mustache or a wig on an individual and still remain true to the story line. Disguising the identity of those we write about, particularly if we're obligated to guard their privacy, is often as easy as changing the name or gender, and switching up a few telling details. Don't think that in order to get to the heart of the story you have to out others.

By the way, have you ever noticed the disclaimer at the beginning of a book? Disclaimers often appear on the copyright page, just before the Table of Contents. You'll see one in this book. Disclaimers make it clear that names have been changed to protect the innocent and they usually read something like this: "To protect privacy, pseudonyms have been used and certain characteristics have been disguised in the case histories recounted." That Bob you think you recognize from Misspellers Anonymous, well, I'm sorry, but that's not the same Bob.

Without employing a disclaimer, writers can also put names in quotes to indicate that this is not the real name. In other words, "Bob" is clearly not Bob from your therapy group.

Here's where things can get tricky. If you're writing memoir, it's pretty hard to camouflage the identities of key players in your life. You can change his name to "Bob" and throw a cowboy outfit on him, but we all know you're describing your alcoholic father, or that brother who ended up in prison. You can't fool us, or them. And rare is the family member who'll take kindly to your version of the truth, or to having their secrets revealed.

It would be great if you could leave these "sensitive" people off the page, but they're likely a major driving force in your story. Come to think of it, you probably wouldn't be telling this story if it weren't for them. Hey, as the author, Anne Lamott once joked, "If people wanted you to write warmly about them, they should've behaved better. "

I once had a lovely, wise professor who spent some time addressing this matter. "If you write about a person," he said, "tell the truth, and do it with love and compassion." To show what he meant, he read a scene from one of his books in which he described, in gorgeous language, the boy he once was, his drunken father, and the abyss between them. After he was done, I cried because I recognized myself. I understood each of the characters, what they wanted yet couldn't have. I felt their pain and love.

This is a good time to mention that great writing is about telling the truth. To have a shot at producing something good, you've got to write down the stuff you swore you'd never tell another living soul. You've got to get it all down, no matter how whiney you sound, or bitter. I promise you, during the process the story will soften on the page. You've got to tell the truth as you see and understand it. If you don't tell the truth, your story will be dead in the water. You'll have to take your manuscript into the backyard and bury it because political correctness only serves to keep your reader at arm's length. They won't be sure what to think or feel, which will only make them bail. You've got to write as if no one will ever read your words. You've got to trust that you're safe. It's not like your words are going to be published tomorrow, anyway.

A word of warning: While you write, when you're most vulnerable to criticism, protect yourself by keeping your manuscript to yourself. Don't foist it onto friends and family members. Do NOT ask for their opinion. This is the single most effective way to shut yourself down. First of all, some ideas shouldn't be shared until you've had the time to reconsider them, to develop them, to allow them to soften so they don't read like psychotherapy rantings. Secondly, you may get your nose out of joint by their lack of enthusiasm. If you're lucky.

Which leads me to this point: Not everybody is your audience. Your kids, your parents, your second cousin twice removed, some of your friends, may not like what you have to say. They may criticize you, and that's OK. It's normal to feel defensive. It takes guts to face into that. But after you've thought about a chapter in your life, examined it from several different angles, reconsidered certain events a thousand times, the need to justify your position will begin to dissipate. Especially when you recognize that your real audience is desperately waiting for you to put into words what they're feeling, what they're yearning to hear. That what they need most of all is your truth. As the author Richard Bausch once said, "There are people out there suffering the wounds and sorrows and terrors of existence who do not have the words to weather it, and it is the writer's place to give expression to that part of experience—to provide a sense of what Joseph Conrad called the 'solidarity of the human family,' and to give forth nothing less than the knowledge that no one, in the world of stories and of art, is ever totally alone."

Perfectionism: The Other Kiss Of Death

Here's a fear-based obstacle I want to take a whip and a chair to. It's a nasty critter. In fact, this might be the biggest challenge you'll face when writing your book, regardless of genre. It's at the very core of why I encourage you to write the shittiest first draft possible, to make that your goal. This obstacle is perfectionism.

Perfectionism is what stops you from putting the first words you think of down on paper for fear of making a mistake. It's what stops you from choosing the next bit to work on because it may take you down a rabbit hole. It's what makes you doubt the worthiness of your whole project, and, worse, yourself.

With perfectionism at the helm, you can't see around your own inadequacy. Instead of typing away, you wring your hands and sob. Just like my daughter, Iman.

Brené Brown wrote a beautiful book on this very topic called *The Gifts of Imperfection*. I encourage you to run, not walk, to the nearest bookstore to buy it. Better yet, order it from Amazon. Until you've got it in hand, I'd like to offer you some of her liberating words.

- "The thing that is really hard, and really amazing, is giving up on being perfect and beginning the work of becoming yourself. "

- "Where perfectionism exists, shame is always lurking. In fact, shame is the birthplace of perfectionism."

- "Perfectionism is not the same thing as striving to be your best. Perfectionism is NOT about healthy achievement and growth. Perfectionism is the belief that if we live perfect, look perfect, and act perfect, we can minimize or avoid the pain of blame, judgment, and shame. It's a heavy shield. We think it will protect us, but it's the thing that's really preventing us from taking flight."

- "Perfectionism is not self-improvement. Perfectionism is, at its core, about trying to earn approval and acceptance."

- "Listen: When failure is not an option, we can forget about learning, creativity, and innovation."

The truth is, we all share the shame-based fear of being ordinary. We're all worried that once people read our book, they're going to see us for the sham we are. If the proof is in the pudding, we don't want to hand folks a spoon.

But I'm not even asking you to be ordinary here. I'm asking you to dare to be shitty. As shitty as shitty can be. I'm asking you to write a draft you'd be ashamed to show your dog. You'll fix what needs to be fixed later, my love. There's plenty of time. Dare to be shitty so you can grow into this writing thing unburdened by perfectionism. To free yourself from its shackles, you need only remember what readers are looking for from you in the first place: connection. In order to connect, you need to let yourself be seen. You need to be imperfect and real; because to be otherwise is so last year.

CHEW ON THIS

1. Create a title for your book.

2. Make a list of all of the people you promise to offend with your writing; then take the list out into your backyard and burn it.

3. Write a disclaimer.

4. Buy and read Brené Brown's book, *The Gifts of Imperfection*.

CHAPTER SIXTEEN

Lordie, I Have No Idea How To Write

I want to pause for a moment and specifically address those of you writing novels or memoirs or any other demanding genres. (Yes, again!) And then I'll focus on the rest of you beautiful, disturbed people.

By now you've likely discovered something very important and very troubling. You've recognized that to some degree you have no idea what you're doing.

Maybe you're clueless as to how to write dialogue. Maybe you're not quite sure how to express inner thoughts, or to work in body language. Or maybe you've got talking heads for thirty pages, and you can't get your main characters away from the kitchen table. There they sit, yakking about the past, waving their silly coffee mugs in the air.

Seems you haven't even gotten going yet, and you're up to your armpits in technical difficulties. These only serve to compound your emotional problems.

Congratulations. That's wonderful news! Because, before you started this project, you had no idea what you didn't know. It all looked so damn easy. You've now graduated to an entirely different level. You've discovered that, to move forward, to finish your first shitty draft, you're going to have to learn a little something about the writing craft.

If you've chosen this type of project because you want to create something beautiful, you'll need to settle in for the long haul and develop some skills. You've already decided that you don't need to finish the project overnight. You're not looking for a resume builder, or professional credibility, or a million dollars. You want readers to clutch your book to their chests and sigh a lot.

That being said, you'll need to sit down, take a deep breath, and remind yourself from time to time that you've taken on a really big tree. Patience, Darling, because once you get that oak into the water, damn, it's going to be great. You may not know this now, but you're going to love this learning thing.

Help Me, Rhonda

It's helpful to know that obstacles are part of the process, but how are you supposed to deal with them when they raise their ugly heads? What can you do if you're confused, say, about setting, or plot, or the relevance of that stuff for your chosen genre? And where do you go for feedback when you really need to know if what you've got is any good?

All writers learn and do at the same time. Don't think for a minute that you need to put your project on hold until you've earned an MFA. To save you the $30,000, I'd like to share with you what I learned at Harvard; the very thing each writing teacher pronounced at the start of the semester: "There is a school of thought that writing cannot be taught. Writing is learned by doing. When you write a lot, you get good." I'd like to modify that expensive statement a bit: We learn something best when we actually need to use it.

Mind you, enrolling in an MFA program is a terrific way to learn how to write, but there are some other ways to develop your craft while working on your book:

Get a coach. If you'd like more personalized, one-on-one attention, lots more focus on your work as you push forward with the process, there's nothing better than hiring a writing coach, like me. Coaching usually entails weekly or monthly sessions—either in person or on the phone—designed to answer your questions, keep you on track, support your mindset, and tweak your writing along the way. Coaching is also about accountability. Enter into a coaching relationship and you'll be browbeaten into producing material on a regular basis. (I so love this part of the coaching process!)

Take an online class. Two or three times a year, I run a six-week, online course that covers important elements of writing including plot, character, conflict, dialogue and setting. And, as hard as this is to believe, I'm not the only show in town. Plug in the keywords "online writing" and see what pops up in your search engine. You'll want to look for a class that provides instruction as well as the discussion of participants' work.

Find a writing class at a local college. College classes are conducted in much the same way as the online variety. Teachers present an aspect of craft, assign readings for better understanding, then have students read aloud from their work to allow everyone, including the author, to hear what works well, and what sounds off. The teacher and fellow classmates then offer their opinion about the work; always looking for ways to solve problems, not tear it down. This is a wonderful way to meet more writers. Remember, the more writers you know, the more you write.

Join a writers' group. These are groups that meet weekly, or monthly, to share their work. Some writers' groups are private, meaning by invitation only. (Don't wait to be invited, form one of your own.) Many are open to the public and are hosted by local libraries or bookshops. Public groups can be interesting because new people show up on a regular basis. Sometimes more experienced writers will help out the newbies, sometimes not. Sometimes, just listening to people share their work and hearing what others have to say about it can be a big help. Can't find one? Check out your local coffee shop, the newspaper, meetup.com, and university bulletin boards.

Join a local writers' workshop. The difference between a group and a workshop is that one is free and unorganized; the other costs money and is structured like a university class. Local workshops are usually less expensive than university workshops, yet they offer the same type of instruction, feedback, and motivation. There's nothing better than having your work closely reviewed by a teacher who understands writing; who can offer his or her observations or ask the right questions to keep your creativity flowing.

Read books on craft. Each time I read about craft, I spot something I want to teach, and to work on in my own writing. Last week, for instance, I read, "Never say, 'I felt, I feel…' in your manuscript. This is not therapy. Show how you felt. Reveal it in an interesting way, but for God's sake, don't start your sentence with I feel." Now I'm going to tear apart my manuscript looking for these phrases to cut. After I tell my students to knock it off.

My favorite craft book, particularly for those who are just getting started, is Anne Lamott's *Bird by Bird*. (There's a reason I quote her so much.) She has a wonderful, funny way of breaking down the main components of the craft and really simplifying them. Her supporting examples always make me roar.

Read other authors. Read like you've never read before, particularly books in your chosen genre. Read to solve your own problems. Analyze how other writers solve that same sticky issue. If you're writing a novel, for instance, read to study the structure; the way the author uses setting, or body language; the balance between action and dialogue; or whatever you need to learn most at any given point in time. Decide if you like the choices an author has made, or not. You get to be the judge. You also get to be your best teacher.

Read *The New York Times Book Review.* *The Book Review* is essentially a series of free tutorials in which professional writers critique the work of each other. I like to think of these reviews as free writing lessons from blunt people. Reviewers describe—in often stunning detail—what makes a recently published book powerful, or lyrical, or what makes the thing a complete disaster, suitable only to line a birdcage. Believe me, these people don't pull punches.

Occasionally, I'll come across a review that describes an issue within a book that I, too, have been struggling with. I'll read on and see how the reviewer thinks the problem could've been solved, and, violá; I've got myself a free writing lesson.

By reading the review, I also get lots of ideas for my own writing. I'm amazed at how creative people are.

AN ASSIGNMENT FROM YOUR COACH

Identify your biggest issue at the moment. Are you having problems describing your characters? Do they sound like Mexican bandits instead of little old ladies? Do your scenes feel unintentionally overwrought, melodramatic? How are you going to attack this issue? Where are you going to learn HOW to fix it? Choose one of the methods above. Do your research; then pull the trigger. Register for the class; or buy that book.

And while you're at it, read this week's *New York Times Book Review.* Underline useful ideas or helpful comments. Take a few notes in your story notebook. How might you use these insights to sharpen your writing?

Do I Need To Worry About This Stuff?

Inspirational books, how-to books, and the like, don't rely as heavily on craft techniques as a novel or memoir. You don't have to keep the narrative smooth over the course of the storyline, or figure out how to transition from one point in time to the next, because the frame of your book doesn't require that. You don't need a narrative arc with a beginning, middle, and end. Your story doesn't depend on action, or conflict, or change. Your job is different. Your tree is smaller. Easier to fell, and pull into the river.

Your job is to tell stories AND clarify a point. Sometimes you have the lesson at the beginning of the chapter, sometimes, the story. You must, however, have both. You also need to give us faces. We need real people to ground us; otherwise we register next to nothing, no matter how terrific the information.

You'll discover that there are far fewer classes geared towards writing books of this sort. You'll likely find writers' groups of little use because their members are used to giving feedback on novels or creative non-fiction with a narrative arc.

Therefore, your best bet is to read other books of this genre. You'll want to analyze how effectively a writer tells a story, makes a point, then supports it with examples or evidence. If something bores you, what mistakes has the author made? If something holds your interest, and you cry, or you truly understand something new, how has the writer created that experience? What is the story/point balance?

CHEW ON THIS

1. Decide what your biggest issue is and how you're going to attack it.

2. Read this week's *New York Times Book Review*. Underline useful ideas or helpful comments.

3. Cry, scream, beat your chest with your fists, eat way too much pie, or take up chain smoking. That's the best way to deal with frustration. NOT!

CHAPTER SEVENTEEN

Untangling The Christmas Tree Lights

Let's say you've FINALLY got yourself a complete first draft. Well, then, congratulations. Pat yourself on the back. You've just accomplished what 95% of the folks who set out to write a book fail to do. This game is about pushing forward come hell or high water. It's about being OK with writing crap for a very long period of time. It's about ignoring your inner perfectionist and managing your doubts and impatience. It's about trusting that you'll iron out the wrinkles when the time comes.

You'll know when your shitty first draft is done when you've written all the stories that you can think of and you have a general idea what the book is about. When you have your stories arranged according to your outline.

You may be fidgeting in your seat right now because you recognize that your book isn't really a book yet. It has no flow to speak of, even though you've done everything you've been told to do. Nothing seems to fit quite right; there's no sense of cohesion.

It's hard not to worry. What if you've wasted all that time and energy for nothing? What if your project persists in looking like a steaming mound of ca-ca?

Hush, my pretty. A first draft is just the stuff you're going to use to create your book, nothing more, nothing less. At this point, it's not a novel, or a memoir, or a motivational book, or whatever it is you decided to write. The very best it can be at this point is a good slab of clay. And that's perfectly OK.

Welcome to the revision process.

Revision is a lot like untangling a solid ball of Christmas tree lights. When you first approach the mess, lying there on the floor just beneath the tree you're supposed to adorn, it seems unsalvageable; a gigantic waste of time and effort. Who the hell throws lights into a box like that?! Collapsing, you scan the room looking for someone, anyone, whom you can blame. But then you spot a single plug head sticking out. You grab hold of it, jiggle it, and lo and behold, one of the wires loosens up. Weaving the plug head in and out, suddenly the mass doesn't seem so impenetrable after all. An entire string separates from the whole. Armed with newfound patience, you tackle the bugger one string at a time until you've got them all lined up ready to go. Problem solved.

Your next job will be to craft the piece you've just created: to identify the problem spots and come up with possible solutions (they never seem to end!), to cut away what isn't necessary, add what is, shape it, develop it, and perfect it. In other words, you'll begin to rearrange the stories, glue them back together again, pull out the excess material, and fill in the gaping holes. You'll begin to put order to the mess. Just like those stinking Christmas tree lights.

But where do you start? What do you look for? How do you know what's useful? What needs to be cut, then tossed into The Spare Brick Pile, that special file you created to house the bits you're not quite ready to throw away?

I could write a whole book on the revision process alone, but for our purposes, I'd like to mark out the basic dance steps you can follow, first for simpler types of books, then for those more complicated. (By the way, in the next chapter, I'll show you where you can go for help when you've done all that you can do. If you need to publish your book sooner rather than later, then feel free to jump ahead.)

Before we dive into the topic of revision, however, I'd like to emphasize something verrrrryyyyyy important: The first shitty draft is not the time nor place to make the decisions we're about to discuss. Your job during that stage is to write your heart out; to explore; experiment; write badly, stupidly, and boringly. Because that's the only way to discover what you have to say. As my friend and business partner Anne Batterson says, "Don't let your editing self get control at this point. (S)he'll zap your energy, make you doubt yourself, make you spend hours diddling around with a sentence, make you feel like a jerk."

Clean Up On Aisle Nine: Revision For Simple Genres

If you're writing a book that doesn't require a narrative arc—motivational, self-help, or how-to, to name just a few—revision will be relatively straightforward. The structure of your book is much less involved. You don't have to keep the same characters moving in and out of your story, or create enough plot points to drive the momentum forward. You don't have to worry about tying individual scenes together into one neat package. You're dealing with teaching points, stories, and the balance between these two.

AN ASSIGNMENT FROM YOUR COACH

During your writing blocks, read through your manuscript one chapter at a time. For each chapter, ask yourself the following questions:

1. What's missing?

2. Is the teaching point unclear or nonexistent?

---

3. Is there a supporting story?

4. Does this story actually support that point?

5. In the story, does the narrative run flat? Do I need more sensory details, or a clear setting, or more dialogue?

Then, once you're satisfied with your individual chapters, ask yourself what's missing from the whole. Have you forgotten an important idea? Have you skipped over a vital step? Identify the hole; then sift through your Spare Brick Pile to see if you've got something that could fill that gap. Do you need to create something better from scratch? If so, do it.

Perhaps you've created some redundancies you weren't aware of. Chapter Seven and Twelve say essentially the same damn thing. Sure, the supporting stories are different, but not the points. Can you harvest the best bits from each and build a single, stronger chapter? Or is it easier to keep one, and ditch the other? Make a decision and act.

You'll also need to make sure you have a compelling introduction. We need to know who you are, why you're offering us this information, and what it means for us, your readers. And at the end, you'll need to draw a conclusion. What does the sum of your points equal? What, when it's all brought together, does it mean? Why does it matter? How does it impact us?

In all likelihood, if your story feels lifeless you've forgotten about story. You must create feeling with things, images, and faces. That flat thing you may be sensing is the lack of emotion.

I love what author Richard Bausch says on this subject, and I'll paraphrase: There is so much more in an image, a face, because that is how we experience the world. A good story is about experience, not concepts and certainly not abstractions. The abstractions are always empty and dull no matter how dear they may be to our hearts and no matter how profound we think they must be. Tell us about a person. Let us be with him or her as they experience the world. Get rid of all those places where you are commenting on things, and let the things stand for themselves. Be clear about the details that can be felt on the skin and in the nerves.

Girding Your Loins: Revision For Novels And Memoirs

For those of you working on a book with a narrative arc, I'm going to break down the revision process further during the next few sections because it's more complex. We'll start off looking at the big picture; then we'll taper down to some of the more important details, which is essentially how you'll direct your attention while working on subsequent drafts.

As I've touched on before, narrative arc refers to the chronological construction of plot in a story. This is a fancy way of saying that every story needs to have a beginning, middle, and end with lots of stuff going on throughout. There are many ways to shape narration: time, juxtaposition (what scenes you place next to the other), a weave of the present and the past, thematic material, and so forth and so on. But the most important aspect of structure, particularly of a novel or memoir (which are both one long continuous story), is the arc. During the rewrite, you'll be arranging your bricks together in such a way as to create this arc.

Oh, stop worrying! You know what an arc is. You see it all the time in architecture, unless you live in a cardboard box, or on some deserted island. There's the Azadi Tower in Tehran, for instance, and the Arc de Triomphe in Paris, and the Gateway Arc in St. Louis. An arc, by definition, is a structure that spans a space and supports structure and weight above it. It's lowest at the beginning and the end, and tallest in the middle. This is the shape of stories, too, and it has been for thousands of years. The arc of the narrative is what keeps the reader turning pages because it's designed to build and maintain suspense in a story. This is the shape they've come to expect, and they get really miffed when they don't find it.

So, how do you create an arc for your book? Simple, at least in concept. You start out with some characters with a set of problems, ramp up the complications until they come to a head, then resolve these complications, or have your characters come to a new understanding of them.

Not only does your book need an arc, so do your chapters. Change has to happen in every chapter, which means there must be some kind of conflict or tension or question presented that gets resolved to some degree (enough to end the chapter but not enough to satisfy the reader, unless you want them to stop reading.) Change has to happen in each scene as well, even those used to present backstory, or we, your readers, won't know why it's there. Change is what creates the arc, drives the narrative, and keeps the reader turning pages. That's the goal, my little beaver.

Narrowing In On Trouble Spots

Now that you've got your bricks mortared together in an effective way, you should feel pretty damn good. (Go back to Chapter Nine if you can't remember what I mean by mortar.)

But you don't.

Are there too many bricks, you ask yourself, too much mortar? Do my scenes show what I hope they do, or do I need to explain with more exposition? Are there big gaping holes that I'm not seeing? Will my readers wonder what happened to that mysterious husband I introduced in Chapter Two?

In other words, you're plagued by questions. You contemplate calling your therapist.

It's time to get to the heart of your project. This draft (and perhaps the next ten) is all about development.

AN ASSIGNMENT FROM YOUR COACH

Read through your manuscript with the eyes of a stranger. Where does your manuscript seem to slow down? What paragraphs, pages, chapters, or scenes don't contribute to the thematic material or the arc? As you read, ask yourself the following questions:

1. Does the story move logically from the first sentence to the last?

2. Are there long passages where nothing happens in real time?

3. Do the main events in my story take place in summary (exposition) or in scenes?

4. If I have too much narrative summary (exposition), which sections do I want to convert into scenes?

5. Could a scene be used to flesh out a major character's personality?

6. Does any of my narrative summary (exposition) involve major plot twists or surprises that would be better served with a scene?

7. Do I have enough narrative summary (exposition), or am I bouncing from scene to scene without pausing for breath?

Once you've read through the entire manuscript with these questions in mind, then added or subtracted what you believe to be necessary, you're going to move on to the next assignment.

Hugging Your Inner Perfectionist

You're going to start making some harder decisions during this next phase of revision. Open the door and let the editor in with her clippers to cut and trim and shape your piece until it's perfect. You heard me right. Unleash that inner perfectionist, the one you've been keeping under lock and key. Perfectionism kills creativity, but she has a place when it comes to the knit-picky stuff some of us (me) would rather ignore.

AN ASSIGNMENT FROM YOUR COACH

Once you're "happy" (notice the quotation marks) with the shape and content of your book, read your piece aloud, sentence by sentence. Yes, this may take a while. You'll hear the awkward sentences when you do this, as well as the tonal changes in the narrator's voice and the places where there's way too much exposition (telling). You'll pick up the clichés, the overused expressions, and the adverbs that need to be doused in gasoline and burned. Do this slowly, chunk by chunk, taking a break every time you lose focus. If you're in charge of putting young children to bed, why not kill two birds with one stone by using your manuscript as a bedtime story? Sure, you may over stimulate the little darlings with your riveting tale, have them bouncing up and down like sugar fiends, but at least you'll know if you're on the right track.

Take a tropical vacation between assignments. Order lots of umbrella drinks. Think about that wonderful Christmas tree light metaphor.

AN ASSIGNMENT FROM YOUR COACH

Read through your manuscript in one or two sittings in order to get really clear on what your book is about. Write a paragraph, not more than a third of a page, summarizing it, pinpointing your themes. This, by the way, is the sort of information you might put on the back cover of your book. (It's also really helpful when penning a synopsis, which we'll talk about later in Chapter 20.) This exercise is usually ridiculously hard to do, but tough it out. There's a reason Mark Twain said, "If I had more time, I would have written a shorter letter." Concise takes work.

With this summary in mind, go back though your manuscript chapter by chapter, cutting everything that doesn't really add to the central theme of your story. (This is a bear, too.) Add scenes that will strengthen and support your theme, or develop as fully as possible those you consider key.

Check into rehab. Check out.

The Bottom Drawer

See how short this section is? Well, that's because it's important. That's the reason I'm separating it out.

When you think you're done with your masterpiece, grab it and stick it in a drawer. Leave it there for at least three months. This allows you the distance to see what you've really got. Each time you revise your piece, you'll be convinced of its brilliance, of its "doneness," because you'll have just blasted out some major veins of junk. But, until your work passes the drawer test, chances are you'll need at least one more major pass. And that's OK. It really is. This isn't a race.

I know that this all sounds like a lot. It is. And I bet you're tired. You should be. I've just given you a load of information without a single supporting story. But I want to remind you that writing is all about taking it bite-by-bite, assignment-by-assignment, step-by-step, page-by-page, and day-by-day. The revision of multiple drafts is all part of the normal process, particularly if your aim is to create something beautiful. There's a good reason most masterpieces take years to write. Those authors weren't just drunken malingerers. It'll all come together if you stay at it, though. I promise.

CHEW ON THIS

1. Reread this chapter. It's one gigantic checklist.

2. Identify the problem spots in your manuscript. Go from big picture to little details.

3. For each major problem, make a list of possible solutions.

4. Choose the solutions; then implement them.

CHAPTER EIGHTEEN

Where To Go When You're Blind

By now you're probably saying, "Great, Ann, I've done all that revision stuff. And I've had it up to here with this tree because it's not coming down. Something's wrong, I think, but I don't know what."

It's easy to go blind to what you've got in hand. You've been looking at the same arrangement of words for so long, you don't know if you've created a best seller, or a more polished mound of crap. Without the necessary distance, it's hard to trust your own judgment. And it's not like your cat can read over your manuscript and give you useful feedback, even if it would like to.

When you're convinced that you've done all that you can do, when you're chomping on the bit to get your book published, whom can you turn to, who can save you from your own impatience and/or enthusiasm?

When I came out of writing school, my classmates and I often analyzed each other's work. One of us would mail her completed piece to the others, then wait a month or two for the package to be returned with a list of problems and recommendations spelled out in red ink. This editorial process took a very long time to complete, but we knew that if we did it for one, the favor would eventually be returned in kind. More importantly, we respected each other's opinions and skillsets, having witnessed them in writing workshops. We weren't just pals who'd met in some seedy bar. Which leads me to my next point: Don't ask your hairdresser, or your best friend from third grade, or your Aunt Earleen to analyze and critique your manuscript. Unless they work for Simon & Schuster, they likely won't be particularly discerning or useful. Even if you're blessed with writing buddies, don't hand them a 300-page manuscript to edit unless you can return the favor, or promise them one of your kidneys as payback. Have respect for others and their time, and have respect for your work.

It's time to hand your manuscript over to a professional. Editing professionals—and we're going to talk about some of the different types in a moment—get paid to study your manuscript, point out problems, and, sometimes, offer corrective suggestions. Unlike your mother or girlfriends, these are people who'll have no trouble telling you the cold, hard truth.

If you'd like to avoid the embarrassment and shame associated with publishing ca-ca, I can't recommend the editing process highly enough. As the old credit card commercial states: Editing services? A few hundred bucks. The truth? Priceless!

There are primarily two types of editing services in the publishing world. The first is holistic editing. The second is copy editing.

Holistic Toledo

Just as holistic medicine considers the whole person—body, mind, spirit, and emotions—in the quest for optimal health, holistic editing considers the whole manuscript—structure, flow, style, and tone—with an eye for soundness and readability.

Holistic editors look for the gaps that need filling, scenes that need chopping, and themes that need supporting. They notice if that important character mentioned in the first chapter disappears for two hundred pages, only to magically reappear. They spot the breaks in the narrative perspective, the dialogue that sounds stilted, and the need for backstory. They read for redundancies, inconsistencies, and believability. You get my drift. Their job is to call attention to these things, and make recommendations. Depending on the editor, these recommendations may be very broad—for God's sake, do not think of publishing this yet—or very specific—you may want to get rid of the nursemaid, who serves absolutely no purpose.

With the collapse of the traditional publishing industry, many holistic editors became free agents after losing their positions at the big houses. Where do you find these folks, now that they're roaming the open plains like buffalo? Online. After all, where would we be without Google? Just type "editing services" into your keyword search and see what pops up. Scroll through the offerings. See who appeals to you. Check out the successful projects they've been involved with. Remember, though, just about anyone can hang up a cyber shingle. Be wise. Ask for references before you hire someone.

You're probably wondering how much this type of service costs, how long the process takes. Easy, Trigger, I'm getting to that. Most holistic editors will request a writing sample and a brief summary of your project, including its page length or word count, before they'll agree on a price and a completion date. They'll need to get a feel for the quality of your writing and the complexity of your book before they can estimate the amount of time and effort required to do their job. The rougher the manuscript—meaning the less precise and clear the writing—and/ or the more sophisticated the project—a children's story, for instance, vs. a full-blown novel—the longer it will take, and the more they'll charge. Ballpark costs, and this is a big ballpark for the reasons stated above, run anywhere from a few hundred dollars to three or four thousand. The editing process may take a few days to complete, or several weeks.

Some editors will turn down your project if they're not interested in your subject matter, or if they have little experience with the genre. Others will refuse the job if they have no time, or if they'd have to charge an arm and a leg to sift through writing that's still too raw. Buck up if you get turned down. Be grateful that you've run into someone with the integrity to refuse your money. Don't be afraid to ask for recommendations. Most editors will happily give them.

For those of you working on less involved genres, consider holistic editing a nice option, not a necessity. For those managing a narrative arc, you don't want to skimp in this department. Do yourself a favor; spend the money.

Line By Line

Unlike holistic editors, copy editors will go through your manuscript line by line. These are the folks who'll fix your punctuation, grammar, and spelling. A writer may be skilled at explaining a procedure or depicting a scene, but the copy editor is the one who makes sure the syntax is smooth; that the writing adheres to the conventions of grammar; that the wording is proper and precise, and the punctuation, appropriate and correctly placed. He or she may also suggest some reorganization, recommend changes to chapter titles or subheadings, and identify lapses in logic or sequential slip-ups. Working through your manuscript, a copy editor will make detailed notes about every problem encountered. When you get your manuscript back, you'll likely find a bunch of "red ink" (corrections) in the document, and a long list of queries in the margins.

A query, by the way, is a diplomatic suggestion for fixing an identified problem. For example: "Hey, you might want to consider taking the horns off the dog. Not sure dogs have horns." Or, "Do you really want to say that his balls were blue? Maybe you should change the color." It is up to you, the author, to incorporate the suggested changes, or not.

> **NOTE:**
> This is a good time to point out that this is not a book on grammar or punctuation; but on how to build a book. My intent is to make this material accessible to you, to keep you engaged, so I've kept my style "casual" without particular concern for dangling participles and contractions. Copy editors hate this stuff. You'll want to choose the style that best serves your genre and audience. In other words, you may not want to try this at home, kids.

Because of the detailed, time-consuming nature of the work, copy editing is more expensive than holistic editing. You can expect to pay two to three times as much for the same manuscript. Again, thanks to the collapse of the publishing industry, there are some wonderful professionals out there who can be found on the Internet. Plug in the keywords "copy editors" and see who comes up. As always, it pays to be wary. Ask for references and work samples.

Regardless of the complexity of your genre, or the method you choose to publish your book, you'd be wise to hire a copy editor. If you're aiming to be published by a major house—and we'll talk more about publishing options in the next section—you'll want to provide them with a clean manuscript, one with all of the major bugs worked out, unless you enjoy being snubbed. Even if you self-publish, don't make the mistake of putting half-baked crap out into the world simply because there's no one stopping you from doing so. The goal is to be taken seriously as an expert and/or writer, not illicit pity.

Most of these things are easy to fix. Fix them. Pay the money. Separate yourself from the junk.

> **NOTE:**
> If English is your second language, you'll even-
> tually need to pay for a copy editor, no ifs, ands,
> or buts. There's no simple way around it. Start
> planning and saving for it now.

Ghost Busters

Sometime during the revision process, most writers toy with the idea of hiring a ghostwriter. It's normal to fantasize about someone who can salvage the project and rescue you when you're knee deep in frustration and angst. It really is. A ghostwriter, for those of you unfamiliar with the term, is a professional who'll write your book while listing you as the author. Sometimes ghostwriters remain completely anonymous, thus the moniker. Sometimes they're listed as the co-author. You might notice this arrangement when you pick up a book by someone famous for something other than writing. Take *Tha Doggfather: The Times, Trials, And Hardcore Truths Of Snoop Dogg* by Davin Seay and Snoop Dogg for instance. Mr. Seay, here, is the ghostwriter. He's responsible for composing every single word, for sweating out all of those revisions. Mr. Dogg, well, he's the guy who's famous.

If the idea of a ghostwriter sounds too good to be true, that's because it is. Ghostwriters charge from $20,000 to $100,000 (or more) to write a book. They'll charge you that much, not only because you're desperate enough to pay it, but also because you're buying six or more months of their life.

Still want to go this route? Plug the keyword "ghostwriter" into Google and up they'll pop. It goes without saying that you'll want to check their publishing credits and references before opening up your wallet or signing a contract.

Consider This

Maybe you're done. Maybe after a couple of revisions, what

you've got is good enough. Maybe you don't need to meet a particularly high standard. You don't need to dot your i's, or cross your t's. You need something simple to place in the hands of potential customers, preferably next week. You know your Why and you're acting accordingly.

Then hold on. Forget about editors. Ask your buddy to read over your manuscript for glaring errors. Make sure the bubble over your grouchy cat is really saying what you want it to say. Then get on with your life. Jump ahead to the next section where we talk about publishing.

CHEW ON THIS

1. If you're writing a book with a narrative arc, locate and hire a holistic editor to examine your manuscript, then a copy editor.

2. If you're writing a book without a narrative arc, locate and hire a copy editor.

3. If you're way too cheap to part with the cash, pass your manuscript by a talented and trusted writing friend. Give her something in exchange for her time and effort, like your first-born child.

STEP FIVE

PUBLICATION FOR DUMMIES

CHAPTER NINETEEN

Layout Of The Land

We've been going on and on about the steps you need to take to build a book: choosing a genre, gathering clay, creating bricks (or stories), developing an outline, revising, and even hiring professional help to polish your final draft. Now, my tenacious little beaver, we're going to explore the three most common types of publishing. This is where the tree meets the water. For most of you, this is the outcome you've been after.

Back in the hay day when I went to graduate school, workshop leaders, almost to a one, would forbid students from discussing the publishing process during class. "You're here to learn how to write," they would say, giving us the hairy eyeball from their lectern. "There's no reason to confuse yourself with that sort of nonsense so early in the game." One of my instructors, a young, stocky fellow by the name of Paul Harding, explained that he'd been working on a novel for seven grueling years. He had yet to publish the thing because he'd continually chuck his drafts in the dumpster, then start again from scratch. Harding's goal was to create something lasting and beautiful and because of this, he refused to allow the pressure to publish to influence him. In 2010, years after I'd graduated, Paul Harding won a Pulitzer Prize in fiction for his first novel, *Tinkers*. Proving that, if you want to create a work of art, time and patience will serve you well.

Not all of you have set out to build a Pulitzer Prize winning novel; and that's just grand. Maybe you want to publish a book in order to buttress your expert credentials, or to build your business, or to motivate your audience to take action. Remember, it doesn't matter what your Why is, only that you own it, and operate accordingly.

No need to dodge any hairy eyeballs here. Let's talk about publishing that book of yours and the options available. Know this stuff, and you'll be far less likely to give up and slide your manuscript in the shredder.

I've got great news. You have absolutely nothing to lose. You don't have to shamelessly flirt with unattractive literary agents, or sleep with an editor, or sell your soul to the devil for the chance to see your book in print. Unless, of course, you want to. You get to choose a method of publishing that fits your big Why, that Why you identified for writing your book in the first place. There's no wrong or right choice, there really isn't. Decide what you want, what best suits your needs, then do your due diligence.

Because changes occur on a stunningly regular basis in the industry, I think it wise to give you a simplistic overview of the three main types of publishing available—traditional, partnership, and self-publishing—and the differences between them. Knowing the major pluses and minuses of each makes choosing so much easier.

CHEW ON THIS

1. Review your Why. Has it changed?

2. Accept that, and read on.

3. Jump up and down, scream, because if you're ready to publish, holy crap!

CHAPTER TWENTY

The Big League

Once upon a time—before the success of wholesalers like Amazon and the advent of eBooks—traditional publishing houses were the only game in town. You wanted your book in print; you had to bang on their castle door. Now, of course, that's no longer the case. You don't need to run their gauntlet in order to be chosen one of the lucky few.

For many writers, however, particularly those who've spent years crafting a beautiful book, and/or those seeking the prestige and reach associated with a well-known house, traditional publishing may still be the preferred way to go. Such a writer typically dreams of getting his or her book published by one of the big six publishing firms—Hachette, Macmillan (Georg von Holtzbrinck Publishing Group), Penguin Group, HarperCollins, Random House, and Simon & Schuster—all of whom have the reputation of heavily promoting their authors and getting the best shelf space in all of the big bookstore chains. Sure, there are hundreds of medium-sized and smaller publishing firms out there too, but, as the thinking goes, get in with one of these big boys and you'll be considered a player. A player who can ignore the marketing piece, and get on with what she loves best: writing books.

And while this reputation is still relatively deserved, times have changed. These conglomerates used to have huge sales forces, public relations teams, and design staffs that worked twenty-four hours a day promoting books (and their authors); but then the industry crashed and folks got laid off right and left, and resources were cut to the bare bone. Authors could no longer leave book promotion to the publishers alone; they were compelled to spend a good deal of time and energy touting their books—particularly on social media sites like Facebook and Twitter—in order to remain on those coveted shelves. And believe me, thinking up pithy Tweets can cut into one's writing time.

> ## NOTE:
> Regardless of the way you choose to publish, know this: You will be required to establish, maintain, and grow your social media presence in order to sell some books. There is NO escape. There are lots of books out there that can show you how to do this. Buy one, and study up.

Traditional publishing houses, in theory, still give authors exposure they wouldn't be able to create on their own. Get in with them, and at minimum, they'll submit your book to trade reviewers, make it available in their seasonal catalog, and make it more visible to buyers, like Barnes & Noble, who'll then champion the book to customers. At best (if you're ridiculously lucky, or famous), these big houses will send you, the author, on tour, get you big ad spaces in movie theaters, have you featured in well-known magazines, and get you radio and TV spots. Nowadays, however, this sort of media blitz happens less and less, regardless of who you are.

Scale-downs aside, traditional publishing houses still have a leg up in the bookstore and library arenas because of deep connections and a purchasing system that is easy for buyers to use. Though the stigma on non-traditional publication is slowly lifting, there remains a much stronger trust between these established publishers and store/library buyers. Such trust affords highly visible shelf space for your book, which equals readers and sales.

Secret Agent Man

If you want to go the traditional publishing route, you'll need to hire an agent to represent you. Manuscripts sent directly to a publisher are called unsolicited submissions. They're usually thrown away; unceremoniously returned in a self-addressed stamped envelope; or, if you're lucky, tossed into a slush pile and read, eventually, by a bleary-eyed intern. Unsolicited submissions have a very low rate of acceptance, meaning you have a much better chance of winning your state's Powerball.

How do you find an agent, you ask? Before the advent of the Internet, you could find one by browsing through *The Writer's Market*—an annual catalog that listed agent names, contact information, and specialties. (*The Writers' Market* is currently an online subscription site.) You can now dig up the same information on Google, or in the back of trade magazines, like *Poets and Writers*. Agents can also be tracked down at writers' conferences, where they troll for new talent—writers with MFA's, experienced authors, or that workshop participant everybody seems to be raving about. Many of these conferences facilitate private meetings between agents and attendees, during which the author is expected to pitch his project (give a brief, alluring description so as to make the agent drool, and beg to represent him).

Tracking down an agent isn't the hard part, getting an agent to pay attention to you, well, that's the trick. Even if you miss the chance to pitch in person, to wow her with your knowledge of Dostoevsky and your brilliant white teeth, you can still grab an agent's interest through the query process. A query is a special type of letter that tells an agent who you are, why you're contacting her, what your book is about—in a paragraph or two—and why you think it would sell well in the current marketplace.

AN ASSIGNMENT FROM YOUR COACH

There are hundreds of books out there that can teach you how to write a proper query letter. Buy one, because it's an art form. Plus, it's always helpful to see examples of what to do, and what not to do. (You'd be astounded how stupid people can be!)

After you study the book, write a query letter draft. Tweak the hell out of it. Then go to *The Writers' Market* and find some agents to send it to. Because there's no sense in writing a query letter unless you actually send it to a real, live agent.

If an agent likes what she sees in the query letter, she may ask for a sample of your manuscript and a synopsis. A synopsis is a more detailed summary of your book, including a description of the major themes, which agents use to sell fiction to a publishing house. (Remember when you compiled this information during the revision process? Bet you're glad you did it now.) If the agent likes your synopsis, if she suddenly thinks of the perfect publisher, or an editor who has bought that kind of book in the past, or has mentioned wanting something along those lines, she would want to contract with you to represent your book. (By the way, unless you want to piss off an agent, which makes no sense to me at all, don't send her your whole manuscript until she asks for it.)

If you've written a non-fiction book, your agent will need you to produce a book proposal, even if you've already finished your manuscript. It's not that agents enjoy being demanding and mean, although I'm sure some do, it's just that publishing houses require book proposals from them before they'll agree to a sale. A book proposal is a forty-or-so-page report that includes a description of the current market for such a book, the points of difference, the author's expertise relative to the topic; a summary; and a sample chapter or two.

AN ASSIGNMENT FROM YOUR COACH

Putting together a book proposal is sort of like writing a master's thesis about your book, only more gruesome. In other words, writing a compelling book proposal requires a hell of a lot of skill. If you've been asked to produce a book proposal, you'll want to buy a good instructional book or ten on the subject to do the job right.

Just as you did for your query letter, write a shitty first draft. Tweak it several times. Hire someone to review it, a holistic editor who specializes in book proposals. Then send it to your agent so she can sell your book.

Mind you, some writers manage to sneak into big traditional publishing houses through the back door, meaning without an agent. This includes bloggers who've attracted large audiences; internet celebrities like Justin Halpern, who wrote *Sh*t My Dad Says*; the creators of Internet memes, like *Angry Cat*; retiring sports figures; instant celebrities, such as Snookie; and anyone a publisher feels could produce a book that will sell a lot of copies.

Of course, if you have a large enough platform—meaning a ready-made audience of 30,000 followers or so—a traditional publishing house would show some interest in you, too, with or without an agent. Don't forget, their job is to make money. If you're popular enough, it doesn't matter if you write like a fourth grader. They can always assign you a ghostwriter.

Just so we can dispatch with any last shred of false hope, you could be the next best thing since J.K. Rowling, but if a house doesn't know who you are, if they can't see a viable market for anything you've written, they likely won't give you the time of day.

Show Me No Money

Most writers dream of the day a big publishing house buys their book and turns it into a bestseller. They can picture the check—an ungodly sum with lots of pretty zeros in it—that will allow them to march into their boss's office, slam their fist on the desk, say what's been on their mind for years, and quit that soul-sucking day job. After the whirlwind tour, and the autograph signing, and the appearances on Oprah, they figure they'll buy themselves a quiet beach cottage in Key West, just like Hemmingway, and set to work on their next big project. Ah, yes, the space to breathe and write. Can't you smell the ocean breeze?

Well, things don't tend to pan out quite that way. Let me explain.

You'll get a check up front, all right, in the form of an advance, but only after a whole bunch of negotiation, which is where your agent earns her bread. Your agent, by the way, gets roughly 15% of your earnings to pay for her services; which she no doubt deserves.

Mind you, advances vary greatly between books, with established authors commanding large advances. That means people like J.K. get the big bucks, not you.

Once a work is accepted, the publishing house negotiates the purchase of your intellectual property, better known as your book (and *all* the rights to it), and agrees on royalty rates. The same parties—the house, your agent, and to some extent you—then agree on royalty rates, the percentage of the gross retail price that will be paid to the author, and the advance payment.

Ready for some math? No need to grab your calculator, I'll do the work for you. Royalties usually range between 10-12% of the recommended retail price. An advance is usually 1/3 of the first print run total royalties. Are you scratching your head? Shall I give you an example? If a book has a print run of 5000 copies and will be sold at $14.95 and the author is to receive 10% royalties, the total sum payable to the author if all copies are sold is $7475. The advance in this instance would be roughly $2490, which sort of makes you want to kill yourself. I mean, there goes the cottage.

Most writers never see more money after their advance check because their book typically dies on the shelf. Publish in the summer, and by the time winter rolls around, the publishing house will have moved on to promoting their new line of books. They're no longer interested in yours. *And they own your book; they've purchased all the rights; so there's nothing you can do.* Which, if you're paying any attention at all, is the sense you get early on when they take over control of the cover design, interior design, and title of your work; when they decide where it will be distributed and in what formats, including paperback and hardback; when they decide on the price of the book, the marketing scope, and when your book releases, or gets put out to pasture. You can argue or plead with the publishing house, but they don't have to listen to a thing you say.

Picture yourself tromping around your local Barnes and Nobel, iced Frappuccino in hand, only to discover your precious book in the remainder bin. All those years of hard work, the sweat and tears, and there it is, atop Tori Spelling's face, selling for $1.19.

In summation, if you want to make money with your book, it's best to steer clear of traditional publishing houses. Which is probably OK, because, unless you have a platform of 30,000 people, most of the big boys won't want to know you anyway.

Pick Me, Pick Me

Wait. One last thing: As far as authorial prestige goes—the glory associated with having one's book published by a large, traditional publishing house—it's a slippery slope. Sometimes, without even knowing it, we humans waste years and years waiting for others to choose us from the masses in order to give us a sense of worth, to convince us that we're talented. Which is silly, because these days, we can choose ourselves, eliminating the middleman. We get to show up at the party without an invitation from the popular girl. With this freedom, though, comes responsibility. It's up to us, not the traditional publishing house, to set a high standard for our work. (And if you tend to suffer from delusions of grandeur, hire an editing professional to serve as a reality check.)

CHEW ON THIS

1. Read a book on query letters, then write one.

2. Send your query letter to appropriate agents.

3. For non-fiction books, read a book on book proposals, then write one.

4. Develop a platform of 30,000 people by blogging and living on social media.

CHAPTER TWENTY-ONE

Not Too Hard, Not Too Soft

The good news is that the publishing industry is wide open for people just like you. In between traditional publishing and do-it-yourself online publishing (which we'll get to shortly) is a new form of publishing that pairs industry experts with new authors. Partnership publishing, as it is known, allows for both the author and the house to contribute the skills they are truly best at, and to develop a close, creative collaboration. If you're the sort who expects, no, demands to have a say in how your book looks, when it's launched, how long it'll stay on the market, how it's promoted, then a partnership press may be just the way to go. This arrangement can also be quite attractive to authors who don't want to learn the necessary skillsets to produce a polished book, or track down the necessary experts for hire, as would be required with self-publishing.

Partnership publishers, or partnership presses, are essentially general contractors. They're like those fellows you'd hire to build a new house, who subcontract out certain tasks—painting, electrical wiring, and plumbing—to independent specialists instead of doing it themselves. Partnership presses work with a vetted pool of free agents—editors, interior and cover designers, illustrators, formatters, social media and public relations experts, e-book experts, and printing companies—on a job-to-job basis. Because they want to get hired for additional projects, the subcontractors working on your book will be, for the most part, conscientious professionals, not hacks.

The downside of using a partnership press is that, instead of receiving an advance from the publishing house for the rights to your book, you, the author, are required to pay a fee up front in most instances. This calculated fee is your share of the production costs.

Let's be real. To bring a book to market requires risk. What if, after all that professional editing, and designing, and printing, and binding, and shipping, your book doesn't sell? What if customers just aren't interested in a book about your angry cat, or your childhood in New Jersey, or the outrageous things your father used to say? Who, then, will pay the bills?

In return for taking on some of the house's financial exposure, you, the author, get to take home a much larger cut of the profits for each book sold. This is what partnership is all about. I'll give you a real, live example:

Remember my husband, Walt, and his fantabulous book? Well, when all was said and done, Walt paid $7500 to publish *Journeys on the Edge* with Aloha Press, a wonderful partnership publisher located in Boise, Idaho. In return, when all was said and done, he received 1,000 books, which he sold for $16/copy on his website and in the back of the room during speaking engagements. Selling them all, he made back the money he'd invested and earned an additional $8500. He also receives a royalty check from the publisher each quarter for books sold through them on Amazon, Barnes and Nobel, and at other retail venues.

You do not sell your book rights to a partnership press; you get to keep them. You can reprint your books, market them any way you like, and sell them until the cows come home. Having exhausted his stock, Walt is now doing another print run of a thousand books for roughly $2500. These books are now much cheaper for Aloha to produce because sub-contract work is no longer required, and, like true partners, they're passing down the savings.

Besides the initial financial outlay, there are some other downsides to partnership publishing. Most partnership presses specialize in one type of book—poetry, children's, self-help, romance novels, or motivational, to name just a few—but some seem to welcome anything that crawls through their door. You'll want to be wary of indiscriminate partnership presses because they may compromise your book's reputation. (Think indiscriminate home improvement contractors.) Judge for yourself by checking out their list of recent publications. After all, you don't want bookstores to associate your beautiful work with the rest of the garbage such a house may produce. There's still a hurdle to get books published by partnership presses onto bookstore shelves, even under ideal circumstances. Why make it that much harder for yourself?

Here's another thing. Publish with a partnership press, and you can expect a truckload of books to darken your doorstep. At the outset, it may sound simple to sell 1,000 copies of your masterpiece, but lots of competent authors end up with a mountain of book cartons in their garage. Then their spouses get annoyed because there's no longer space to park the car. And soon marital tension erupts because someone has to go out and scrape the windshield on frosty winter mornings, which wouldn't have been necessary if the damn car hadn't been parked in the driveway to begin with. Remember, the publisher is busy moving their copies of your book, books that will earn you a royalty, so they can't help you offload your stock. That's your job. You'll need to become a pro at book promotion, or hire the task out, not depend on them.

AN ASSIGNMENT FROM YOUR COACH

Book promotion is your new J-O-B. I'm sorry, I know I'm repeating myself, but you can't stop now. If you're not on social media yet, time to get cracking. Join Facebook, Twitter, Pinterest,

Linkedin, and any other up and coming networking site. Poke around; connect with other authors. What are they doing to promote their books? Copy them shamelessly.

If you don't have your own website, build one. Or hire someone to design one for you. Check out elance.com to find a website designer.

Even if you're a wallflower like me (no, seriously!), it's time to put yourself in front of new people and talk about your book. Give a presentation at the local library, Chamber of Commerce, or Rotary Club. Blab with the checkout lady, and your babysitter, and the guy who delivers your newspaper. Slip the waitress your business card—the one with your web address and book blurb—along with the tip. No one is going to trip over your book, and then buy it; you have to lead them to it.

As a final note, I recently ran into an interesting partnership press that caters to motivational speakers. Instead of producing a written draft to work with, these authors record their stories verbally. The company then transcribes the stories and turns them over to a ghostwriter for revision. After the ghostwriter does his thing, the company publishes the resultant book, all for a fee of $25,000.

At first blush, this arrangement sounds attractive, considering the head banging it promises to save; until, of course, you bump into the problem: Most beginners have no idea where to begin, what stories to tell, what points to make, what message they mean to share. Which is sort of what you've had to figure out during the long, drawn out process of writing multiple drafts. A book with a clear message (or theme) doesn't just fall out of the sky; it must be cultivated. By now you'd likely agree.

CHEW ON THIS

1. Find a partnership press with a good reputation.

2. Clean out a space in your garage for book cartons.

3. Develop a platform by blogging, speaking, and tending to social media.

4. Learn to self promote.

CHAPTER TWENTY-TWO

Large And In Charge

Self-publishing, also known as indie (short for independent) publishing, is currently the most common way for new authors to bring their books to market.

Because this is the "easiest" method of publication, I'd like to begin this section with a warning: Without publishing house roadblocks to navigate, agents to win over, or partnership standards to be taken into account, the biggest mistakes an indie author can make is to rush the publication of his or her book, and to scrimp on expert costs. Remember, to complete your first draft, you must embrace the shitty. To publish said shit, however, only serves to soil your family name. To quote Nancy Reagan, just say no.

If you're going to self-publish your book, the one you've spent all that time and effort writing, be wise. Hire a designer and an editor or two to clean up your manuscript. Do what it takes to make it look professional before you toss it into the world. If you're putting out a novel or a work of creative non-fiction, you'll, at the very least, want a holistic editor to identify narrative issues, and a copy editor to fix your punctuation, sentence structure, and grammar. For any other type of book, you'd be well served to hire a copy editor, someone who can save you from looking illiterate.

Now that I've addressed the impulse to just "get 'er done," let me give you an overview.

Self-publishing is all about control, which is great news for us control freaks. Because you don't sell your rights, or enter into a partnership agreement, you, the author, control not only the design and title of your book, but the release date, the price it sells at, reprints, format, marketing, and so on and so forth. This also means that you have to do all of the work as well, or locate and hire professional help. You are the general contractor. If, for instance, you wanted to create an audio book, not just a paperback copy, you'd need to record it yourself with the proper equipment, or hire a voice actor, which, by the way, isn't all that difficult with sites like elance.com around. Even if you secure the services of professionals to do the tasks that you're not equipped to do, or don't want to learn how to do, it's still you who chooses the talent and what the final product will look like. You're the head honcho who takes competitive bids and researches the members of your team by looking at past work and obtaining references, just like you would for any other contract process. In other words you, my dear, are large and in c-h-a-r-g-e.

With control comes financial responsibility. Self-publishing, like partnership publishing, has some upfront expenses. The average cost for a quality product, including an electronic version of your book, is around $1500, most of which goes to a freelance editor. Other costs can include interior and cover design, ISBN purchasing, copyright registration, and purchasing hard copy inventory.

AN ASSIGNMENT FROM YOUR COACH

Buy an ISBN number if your publishing provider does not include one with their services. ISBN stands for International Standard Book Number. This is a unique numeric book identifier, which is assigned to each edition and variation (except reprintings) of a book, i.e., e-book, paperback, or hardcover. This number is country-specific, and in the U.S. you, or any publishing house, can obtain one through the privately held company R.R. Bowker (www. bowker.com). There's a charge for this number, which varies upon the number of ISBN's purchased, with prices starting from $125 for a single number.

Then copyright your book by going online; completing a copyright application; paying a filing fee of $35; and sending the Copyright Office, a branch of the Library of Congress, a copy or copies of your book. The principal intention of copyright records is to document the intellectual or creative ownership of a work. This means that no one can steal your work. You can find lots more information at www. copyright.gov.

(In case you're wondering, you don't need to have a Library of Congress number, which is used as an index for libraries in order to catalog their holdings. Only major publishers deal with Library of Congress numbers.)

Becoming familiar with these aspects of the publishing process can often entail a learning curve. If you don't like learning new tricks, consider the partnership press option. Never forget: Time is money.

Dollars And Sense

That being said, self-publish a book, and the lion's share of the profit will end up in your pocket—usually 60-70% for the paper version of your book when sold through a distributor.

With a few simple formatting changes, your paper book can also be turned into an e-book and marketed on several different sites. Depending on the price of your e-book, you stand to make anywhere from 30-50% or more of those profits. There are a number of indie authors out there making serious bank selling their electronic books on these various sites. They have figured out how to drive sales by adjusting purchase prices, tagging popular authors or books, and studying the ins and outs of the system. And believe you me; some of the more successful ones aren't particularly gifted writers.

Here's another beautiful thing: Your reader can order a book—either the electronic or paper version—directly from Amazon (or from any other online site that produces and markets books), and the company will ship it, collect the money, and send you your profits. Which means that you don't end up with a garage full of books, and the associated marital discord. Now, if or when you need inventory for back of the room sales, you can buy copies from your online wholesaler for a relatively low cost, say, $5 each, which you can then sell for as much as you'd like, usually $15 or more. Remember, it's you, Bucko, not the publishing house, who determines the sales price anyway.

To make money, you actually have to sell books. Because indie authors are 100% responsible for their own marketing, your sales success will be dependent upon how much money and hustling you're willing to put into it. You can't kid yourself: No one out there is doing it for you.

Where To Go When You Want To Self-Publish

Createspace.com is the best-known self-publishing provider currently out there. This company, a division of Amazon.com, provides free tools to help you produce "library-quality" books, professional trade paperbacks, as well as e-books. They offer the use of their "affordable top-notch professional" services, including editing, layout and design, and formatting, so you don't have to beat the bushes looking for your own. If you're not interested in paying these "affordable" fees, you can simply go to the site, register for free, download a FREE template, then copy and paste your manuscript into the template one chapter at a time. They'll also throw in a free ISBN number. If you need help with any of this stuff, a customer service representative will walk you through the process step-by-step.

Then Createspace will distribute your books—both the paper and the electronic Kindle™ versions—on Amazon, personal web sites, and in an "expanded distribution channel," which includes bookstores, other online retailers, libraries, and academic institutions. Through Createspace, the manufacturing and shipping of your book is completely taken care of. Your book remains in stock without inventory, and made on-demand when customers order.

If you're in a hurry, which I really hope you're not, 48hrbooks (www.48hrbooks.com) can help you design your book, produce it, and ship it to you in two days time. They do not, however, involve themselves in the creation of e-books, nor will they market your book online, or satisfy outside orders. If you want an ISBN number, which you do, you can purchase one through them, or go to www.bowker.com. We're talking paper books placed in your hands fast.

Many successful e-book authors have their books separately formatted for Amazon, Barnes & Nobel, Smashwords, and Kobo, which all have slightly different requirements. Such authors go to the trouble and expense for the sake of increased visibility. The e-book industry is a huge marketplace offering authors enormous profits, so you may want to consider investigating these sites as well.

CHEW ON THIS

1. Choose a publishing provider.

2. Hire an editor to clean up your manuscript.

3. Hire an interior designer and a cover designer.

4. Purchase an ISBN number from Bowker.com if your provider doesn't include one.

5. Copyright your book through www.copyright.gov

6. Develop a platform and learn to self promote.

The End, Or The Beginning

I want you to know how honored I am that you've trusted me with your beautiful dream. You've allowed me the privilege of teaching you some of what I know about building a book. I've had the opportunity to sneak in a little writing lesson here and there, which is always great fun; and to talk about what makes a story memorable and powerful. Because, as writers, that's what we want, to create a book readers will value for a very long time. We want our story to matter. We want to move people, to make them feel something, to look at life through different lenses. And that's what our readers want, too. They want to feel right alongside us. They want to learn, to consider their own challenges from a different perspective, our perspective.

You've taken on a big, hairy audacious goal. You've placed yourself, with a knife and fork, before a roasted elephant. With this bite-by-bite plan in hand, however, I know you're up for the task. I'm sure of it.

And here's my promise: By the time you are through, by the

time you sign off on the final draft and publish your book, you'll be a different person. You'll develop confidence as a human being, one with an opinion. You'll become a writer. And more than that, a published author. You'll finally understand your story—and human nature—better than you ever thought possible. You'll become an expert. You'll learn how to endure; how to overcome obstacles, how to stick to a task until you're done, how to discipline your inner beaver.

You have a lot of work to keep you busy. You'll be writing stories—creating bricks—for quite some time. Relax into that. When it's time, when you have a stockpile of bricks, you'll begin putting them into order. You'll fit them neatly into your outline, then stand back and take a good look at what you've got. You'll glue, then re-glue all the pieces together, which is the essence of the revision process. You'll do this for quite some time. And when you think you've got it, when you think it's really good, you're going to turn it over to a professional editor to have a good look. And that editor will likely say, "It's not ready." You'll receive a list of all the things you need to fix; and I want you to take this news like a good beaver. I want you to say, "Hey, now I know how much chewing I need to do to get this log into the water. Hurray!" You'll fix it. And then you'll publish your book; by one of the methods we've talked about here. And it will be good. It will be very, very good. Just like you.

The writer's life can be lonely. You'll have no idea if what you're producing is any good. None of us do. That's simply the way this process works. Reach out for help and instruction. When you need something more, read, take a class, join a writers' group, hire a coach. If you want that trusted safety net, if you want to make absolutely sure that you do what it takes to complete your book, you're welcome to work with me. You can contact me at annsheybani@gmail.com.

Know this, nothing would make me happier than to pass by a bookstore window and see your name on the cover of that brand new, best selling book.

But for now, I wish you great patience; which is so much more important than luck. And I wish you satisfaction and joy.

Appendix 1

STEP ONE CHEWLIST

√ Take out your calendar. Commit to and schedule two 3-hour sessions or three 2-hour sessions this week. You'll be doing this each week for the foreseeable future. Nurture the habit.

√ Buy two notebooks. One for your stories; one for your Morning Pages.

√ Each morning, write three Morning Pages to flush your mental toilet.

√ Each evening, make a few notes in your story notebook to keep your project percolating.

√ Answer this question in sickening detail: I want to write this book for/because…

√ And this one: I want my readers to understand…

√ Choose one genre. There are no mistakes. This is the draft you'll complete.

√   Shop for and buy the book that best represents your vision; one that you'd like to model.

√   Remove one time sink from your weekly schedule so you can create a writing block.

√   Copy these words in black magic marker—the bigger the better: My J-O-B is to write a shitty first draft. Now hang them on the wall next to your computer.

√   Create a Scrap Heap folder on your computer. This is where the stuff you chop will end up.

√   Make a mistake this week. Tell people about it. Notice how you feel. Have a good laugh. Think about how you might do it differently next time.

√   During your scheduled writing block time, gather any material that's useful to your project.

√   Look for common themes and create separate piles for them.

√   Copy these tidbits of material into a Word document labeled *My Fabulous Book.*

√   Browse through blogs on the Internet. Is it time to start your own, as a way of consolidating your message and creating an audience?

STEP TWO CHEWLIST

√   Create a list of writing prompts—ten to twenty of them—that you can turn to when you have no clue where to begin. Keep these in your story notebook.

√ Begin your block times with a 10-minute writing prompt of your choosing. If you're working in non-fiction, write from your perspective about a particular memory. If you're creating fiction, write from the perspective of one of your main characters, even if you don't know him or her very well yet.

√ Check out Amazon.com for writing prompt books. Order one. Play with it.

√ Identify the smallest building block you're going to create, based on your genre. Are we talking blog post? Scene? Case study?

√ Identify the elements of story in your Word document (*My Fabulous Book*). What do you have in spades? What is glaringly absent?

√ Make a list of three stories you'd like to flesh out.

√ Choose one and work on it during block time.

√ Study the balance of story elements vs. straight information in the book you've chosen to model. Does this book have enough sensory details for your taste? Too much? Are there enough faces?

√ Focus on one building brick in the book you've chosen to model. Decide what's missing. How is the balance off, if at all? What would be more satisfying? What sort of details or elements does it use that interest you most? What, if anything, seems to weigh the story down?

√ Determine how much page space this building brick takes up? One page? Two? A half?

√ Make some notes in your story notebook: How much detail will your bricks need? Which story elements? How long should your stories be?

√ Answer the appropriate set of assigned questions in Chapter 8.

√ Regardless of genre, make a list of the words or broad concepts you need/want to explore more fully?

√ Make a list of the faces we're going to see the most?

√ Create a special folder called The Spare Brick Pile. Put things you cut from your document, or aren't sure about, here

√ Take a powerful line from a story you've written. Use it as a writers' prompt and see what develops.

√ Open a book you're reading, preferably the one you've chosen to model. Pick a random page. Find the story. (*Hint: Look for the face.) Decide if the story is complete, or if it gets picked up and expounded upon later in the game.

√ On that same page, just for fun, identify the mortar: the material or device used to connect two stories/scenes together.

STEP THREE CHEWLIST

√ Locate the Table of Contents in the book you've chosen to model.

√ List ten or more words you might use to describe the content of your book, words that you might use in a chapter title.

√ Take out the narrative book you've chosen to model and examine the length and composition of the chapters. Are they filled with setting description, background information, back and forth dialogue? Do the lessons stand out, or are they tightly woven into the storyline?

√ Make some notes about what you'll need in your chapters to serve as a guideline, either in your story notebook, or in the book itself.

√ Or take out the motivational/inspirational book you've chosen to model.

√ Examine the length and composition of the chapters. Are they filled with quotes, lists, bullet points, song lyrics, pictures of cats? Are the lessons clear? Do the stories support the points?

√ Answer this: How is the unique process broken down for the reader? Is it built into a step-by-step structure?

√ Make some notes about what you'll need in your chapters to serve as a guideline, either in your story notebook, or in the book itself.

√ Open the book you've chosen to model and copy the structure of the Table of Contents in outline form on a sheet of paper.

√ If the Table of Contents is too complicated, or non-existent, create a well-spaced, numbered list of 8-15 chapter titles.

√ For each chapter title, write down a very brief description of what it's about.

√ Beneath these descriptions, write a list of the subject areas that will be covered, or the plot points.

√ Beneath these lists, write down five questions your reader will likely ask, then turn these questions into statements.

√ Identify the plot points in one chapter of the narrative

book you've chosen to model.

√ Play The Question Game for each chapter of your novel or memoir (or other narrative genre) to create a more substantive book outline.

STEP FOUR CHEWLIST

√ Create a title for your book.

√ Make a list of all of the people you promise to offend with your writing; then take the list out into your backyard and burn it.

√ Write a disclaimer.

√ Buy and read Brené Brown's book, *The Gifts of Imperfection*, so you can get over your crippling perfectionism.

√ Decide what your biggest issue is and how you're going to attack it.

√ Read this week's *New York Times Book Review*. Underline useful ideas or helpful comments.

√ Reread Chapter 17. It's one gigantic checklist.

√ Identify the problem spots in your manuscript. Go from big picture to little details.

√ For each major problem, make a list of possible solutions.

√ Choose a solution; then implement it.

√ If you're writing a book with a narrative arc, locate and hire a holistic editor to examine your manuscript, then a copy editor.

√ If you're writing a book without a narrative arc, locate and hire a copy editor.

√ If you're way too cheap to part with the cash, pass your manuscript by a talented and trusted writing friend.

STEP FIVE CHEWLIST

√ Review your Why. Has it changed?

√ Read a book on query letters, then write one if you're going the traditional route.

√ Send your query letter to appropriate agents if you're going the traditional route.

√ For non-fiction books, read a book on book proposals, then write one if you've been asked for one.

√ Or find a partnership press with a good reputation.

√ Develop a platform by blogging, speaking, and engaging with social media.

√ Choose a publishing provider if you're going the self-publishing route.

√ Hire an editor to clean up your manuscript if you're planning to self-publish.

√ Hire an interior designer and a cover designer if you're planning to self-publish.

√ Hire a formatting professional or learn the skill if you're planning to self-publish.

√ Purchase an ISBN number from Bowker.com if you're publishing provider does not provide one.

√   Copyright your book through www.copyright.gov if you're planning to self-publish.

Appendix II

BOOKS MENTIONED

The Artist's Way by Julia Cameron

The Go-Giver by Bob Burg and John David Mann

The Little Book of Romanian Wisdom by Diana Doroftei

Life: Selected Quotes by Paulo Coelho

Boundaries Workbook: When to Say No and When to Say Yes by Henry Cloud

The Self-Esteem Workbook by Glenn Shiraldi

The Right Words at the Right Time by Marlo Thomas

A Blessing in Disguise by Andrea Joy Cohen

Simple Grace by Beth Jannery

The Art of Exceptional Living by Jim Rohn

The Secrets of Skinny Chicks by Karen Bridson

Design Your Self by Karim Rashid

Journeys on the Edge: Living a Life that Matters by Walt

Hampton

Own Your Niche by Stephanie Chandler

Feel the Fear and Do it Anyway by Susan Jeffers

Fearless Living by Rhonda Britten

Let's Pretend This Never Happened by Jenny Lawson

*Sh*t My Dad Says* by Justin Halpern

A Walk in the Woods by Bill Bryson

A Year in Provence by Peter Mayle

Eat, Pray, Love by Elizabeth Gilbert

Traveling Mercies by Anne Lamott

Little Bee by Chris Clive

Gone with the Wind by Margaret Mitchell

The Pirate Lord by Sabrina Jeffries

Confessions of a Scoundrel by Karen Hawkins

The Atlantis Gene by A.G. Riddle

The Martian by Andy Weir

The Shining by Stephen King

Joe Dies at the End by David Wong

Never Go Back by Lee Child

Ripper by Isabel Allende

The Walking Drum by Louis L'Amor

The Light of Western Stars by Zane Grey

Interpreter of Maladies by Jumpha Lahiri

Birds of a Lesser Paradise by Megan Mayhew Bergman

Hidden Drive by Chivas Sandage

School of the Arts by Mark Doty

The Hunger Games by Suzanne Collins

Harry Potter and the Sorcerer's Stone by J.K. Rowling

Beezus and Romona by Beverly Cleary

Hello God, It's Me Margaret by Judy Blum

The Rainbow Fish by Marcus Pfister

The Velveteen Rabbit by Margery Williams

Grumpy Cat: A Grumpy Book by Grumpy Cat

The Grapes of Wrath by John Steinbeck

Pride and Prejudice by Jane Austen

Outliers by Malcolm Gladwell

Silence of the Lambs by Thomas Harris

Holy Bible: King James Version by Unknown

Shift your Mind: Shift the World by Steve Chandler

China in Ten Words by Yu Hua and Allan H. Barr

Tuesdays with Morrie: An Old Man, a Young Man, and Life's Greatest Lesson by Mitch Albom

Bird by Bird: Some Instructions on Writing and Life by Anne Lamott

The Alchemist by Paulo Coelho

The Gifts of Imperfection: Let Go of Who You Think You're Supposed to Be and Embrace Who You Are by Brené Brown

Tha Doggfather: The Times, Trials, And Hardcore Truths of Snoop Dogg by Davin Seay and Snoop Dogg

Tinkers by Paul Harding

2014 Writer's Market by Robert Lee Brewer

Appendix III

RECOMMENDED READING

Bird by Bird: Some Instructions on Writing and Life by Anne Lamott

The Artist's Way by Julia Cameron

The War of Art by Steven Pressfield

Do the Work by Steven Pressfield

Bang the Keys: Four Steps to a Lifelong Writing Practice by Jill Dearman

The Situation and the Story by Vivian Gornick

Reading Like a Writer: A Guide for People Who Love Books and for Those Who Want to Write Them by Francine Prose

How to Write a Book Proposal by Michael Larsen

Nonfiction Book Proposals Anybody Can Write by Elizabeth Lyon

The Elements of Style by William Strunk Jr., E.B. White and Robert Angell

Blank to Book: From Idea to Amazon in 150 Days! by Mary-anna Young

Writing Down the Bones: Freeing the Writer Within by Natalie Goldberg.

Query: Everything You Need To Get Started, Get Noticed, and Get Signed by C.J. Redwine

Acknowledgements

Being a die-hard perfectionist, this book would have taken me centuries to finish were it not for my husband, Walt Hampton, who insists on making absolutely everything a competition, including writing and publishing books. For his insufferable gloating, and his ability to make me laugh, I thank him.

I'd also like to acknowledge my partners at East Hill, Anne Batterson and Sherry Horton, who have taught me more about writing than I can shake a clichéd stick at. You can't ask for better friends and mentors.

Last but not least, to my many students and coaching clients who have laid it all out on the page, who have exposed themselves in the most vulnerable way, who have dug deep, who have gone back to the drawing board time and time again, who have remained open to feedback despite feeling pissy, who have created the most beautiful stories; know that I value and respect you.

ABOUT THE AUTHOR

Ann Sheybani is the co-founder of East Hill Writers' Workshops, a supportive community for blossoming writers.

She received her Masters in Creative Writing and Literature from Harvard University. Her blog, Things Mama Never Taught Me, can be found at www.annsheybani.com.

She and her husband, Walt, split their time between Canton, Connecticut and County Cork, Ireland.

You can contact her at annsheybani@gmail.com.